Thousands of Broadways

The Rice University Campbell Lectures

Thousands of Broadways

Dreams and Nightmares of the American Small Town

ROBERT PINSKY

The University of Chicago Press   CHICAGO AND LONDON

ROBERT PINSKY's most recent books of poetry are *Gulf Music* (2007) and *Jersey Rain* (2000). His prose works include *Democracy, Culture, and the Voice of Poetry* (2002) and *The Life of David* (2005). He is also translator of *The Inferno of Dante* (1995) and coeditor of the anthology *An Invitation to Poetry* (2004). Among his honors are the William Carlos Williams Award, the Los Angeles Times Book Prize, the Shelley Memorial Award, the Pen-Voelcker Award from PEN, and the Lenore Marshall Prize. As U.S. Poet Laureate from 1997 to 2000, he founded the Favorite Poem Project. He teaches in the Creative Writing Program at Boston University, and is poetry editor of the online magazine *Slate*.

The University of Chicago Press, Chicago 60637
The University of Chicago Press, Ltd., London
© 2009 by Robert Pinsky
All rights reserved. Published 2009
Printed in the United States of America

18 17 16 15 14 13 12 11 10 09   1 2 3 4 5

ISBN-13: 978-0-226-66944-1 (cloth)
ISBN-10: 0-226-66944-0 (cloth)

Library of Congress Cataloging-in-Publication Data
Pinsky, Robert.
    Thousands of Broadways : dreams and nightmares of the American small town / Robert Pinsky.
        p. cm. — (The Rice University Campbell Lectures)
    ISBN-13: 978-0-226-66944-1 (cloth: alk. paper)
    ISBN-10: 0-226-66944-0 (cloth: alk. paper)
    1. American literature—History and criticism. 2. City and town life in literature. 3. Cities and towns in literature. 4. City and town life in motion pictures. 5. Cities and towns—United States. I. Title.
    PS169.C57P5 2009
    810.9'3587309732—dc22   2008026879

♾ The paper used in this publication meets the minimum requirements of the American National Standard for Information Sciences—Permanence of Paper for Printed Library Materials, ANSI Z39.48-1992.

Their union on the soil of America at once presented the singular phenomenon of a society containing neither lords nor common people, and we may almost say neither rich nor poor. These men possessed, in proportion to their number, a greater mass of intelligence than is to be found in any European nation of our own time. All, perhaps without a single exception, had received a good education, and many of them were known in Europe for their talents and their acquirements. The other colonies had been founded by adventurers without families; the immigrants of New England brought with them the best elements of order and morality; they landed on the desert coast accompanied by their wives and children. But what especially distinguished them from all others was the aim of their undertaking. They had not been obliged by necessity to leave their country; the social position they abandoned was one to be regretted, and their means of subsistence were certain. Nor did they cross the Atlantic to improve their situation or to increase their wealth; it was a purely intellectual craving that called them from the comforts of their former homes; and in facing the inevitable sufferings of exile their object was the triumph of an idea.

Alexis de Tocqueville, *Democracy in America*, Volume I, Chapter II

It was early evening of a day in the late fall and the Winesburg County Fair had brought crowds of country people into town. . . . In the main street of Winesburg crowds filled the stores and the sidewalks. Night came on, horses whinnied, the clerks in the stores ran madly about, children became lost and cried lustily, an American town worked terribly at the task of amusing itself. . . . There is something memorable in the experience to be had by going into a fair ground that stands at the edge of a Middle Western town on a night after the annual fair has been held. The sensation is one never to be forgotten. On all sides are ghosts, not of the dead, but of living people.

Sherwood Anderson, *Winesburg, Ohio,* "Sophistication"

CONTENTS

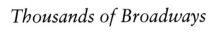

Thousands of Broadways

I {DAWSON'S LANDING}

Puddn'head Wilson, Mark Twain's peculiar allegory about American racial consciousness (and unconsciousness) begins: "The scene of this chronicle is the town of Dawson's Landing, on the Missouri side of the Mississippi, half a day's journey, per steamboat, below St. Louis." Twain's delectable and sly opening sentences describe the "snug" riverside town with its "pretty homes" "almost concealed from sight by rosevines, honeysuckles and morning-glories." Cats drowse among flowerpots. On the one main street, downtown, a striped pole indicates not "nobility proud and ancient" as in Venice, but "the humble barber shop." Outside the tinmonger's, pots and pans hung on a pole jangle their advertisement in the breeze off "the clear waters of the great river"—the Mississippi, that "washes" "the hamlet's front" and brings the lively riverboat traffic to the unruffled town, backed by its crescent of hills "clothed with forests from foot to summit."

This opening spins a dream of real estate, and of a serene communal shelter, glowing with Twain's ability to enjoy the idyll while also laughing at these summery or springtime surfaces, too blandly good to be true, vivid and all but convincing. The narration, along with the master raconteur's joy in setting up his audience for a punch line, genuinely admires this thriving, slumberous little place, as well. The deceptively even surface of the language—reflecting the deceptive surface of the town—acknowledges Twain's own ambivalence.

Here is Main Street as it might dream of itself, its commercial life resembling a stressless and even protective extension of nature, the hills "clothed" in forest, the whole scene practically a garden, the town augmenting the river and hills and trees with no visible evidence of sweat or violation:

> All along the streets, on both sides, at the outer edge of the brick sidewalks, stood locust-trees with trunks protected by wooden boxing, and these furnished shade in summer and a sweet fragrance in the spring when the cluster of buds came forth. The main street, one block back from the river, and running parallel with it, was the sole business street. It was six blocks long, and in each block two or three brick stores three stories high towered above interjected bunches of little frame shops. Swinging signs creaked in the wind, the street's whole length.

After opening his novel with four leisurely paragraphs elaborating this unrippled pastoral, Twain writes these curt sentences:

Dawson's Landing was a slaveholding town, with a rich slave-worked grain and pork country back of it. The town was sleepy and comfortable and contented.

Those honey-slow introductory paragraphs need to appreciate the modest, fragrant tranquility of the sleepy riverfront Eden, in order to emphasize the coming story's generating presence and agent: the concealed, profit-generating Serpent of race. Any horror at the town's complacent blindness is so understated that the writer's narration itself might seem unaware. The three concluding adjectives, "sleepy and comfortable and contented" are qualified by an almost-imperceptible irony—a soft, hand-rubbed sheen of misgiving, applied by that extended, lyrical description of the creaking signs above shop doors, the cats drowsing among flowerpots, the protective boxing around the locust trees.

Twain's understatement about slavery, here at the end of his mellow-seeming prelude, creates a drama of expectations: how severe is that nearly invisible irony, if it is there at all? How terrible will that Serpent of slavery prove to be in this drowsy, thriving little Paradise, and to what extent does the bland surface of unawareness make the Serpent all the more muscular and implacable?

Twain's flawed, cranky, and audacious book, realistic in texture, resembles a fable or joke in structure. I read it early in my life, and re-read it, maybe in part for the waterfront town—my copy came from the Long Branch Public Library on Broadway, the main street of my own Jersey Shore home town, the library a few blocks west of the beach painted by Winslow Homer, and a mile or two south of the Shrewsbury River.

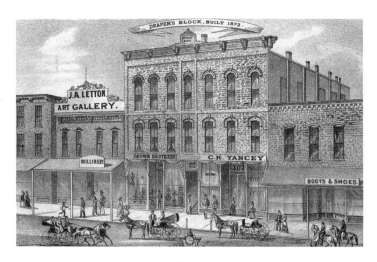

FIGURE I. Broadway in Mark Twain's childhood home town of Hannibal, Missouri, ca. 1875: decades before he wrote *Pudd'nhead Wilson* and decades later than the book's antebellum, slave-state setting. Used by permission of State Historical Society of Missouri, Columbia.

I appreciated the unfolding of *Puddn'head Wilson*'s racial detective story, which Twain hinges on the new art of fingerprinting. I think the story may have made me permanently a believer in nurture over nature. If I recognized Twain's portrait of small-town life, along with that ambivalent picture of charm and corruption, I possibly also recognized Twain's understanding of a genial, defensive American impatience with politics and political ideas—with all ideas, with the past itself. The communal organism he presents cannot see beyond its own appetites and responses. His characters enact decisively the horror of that sleepy, contented blindness. The white citizens of Dawson's Landing execute a paradigm of the race-based slave culture, its contradictions and hypocrisies, and Twain has them dance that lethal pattern to a tinkling, comic music.

6

The central character called Tom (not his birthname) is one thirty-second black, a fact Tom himself is unaware of until he is an adult: traumatic, fatal knowledge that the spoiled young white man desperately conceals from Dawson's Landing. When his privileged place in the race system is threatened, Tom's response is not to question the system but to deceive it by preserving his privilege at all costs—including murder.

Tom is one of two infants, one white and one black, who were switched in the cradle by Tom's real mother, the slave Roxy. Twain never quite says that the boys are half-brothers. Like Tom, Roxy is fair skinned and light haired, living evidence of slavery's sexual component: a reality that the town must both deny and accommodate. In keeping with the surface of mores that suppress the sexual reality, Roxy of course speaks like a slave, while her son Tom speaks and behaves like a privileged brat. (Roxy's intelligence and character, it turns out, are much superior to her son Tom's, a fact that Twain's rendering of her dialect makes the more poignant.)

In Twain's emphatic triumph of social environment over heredity, the slave infant Tom has grown up to become an arrogant, criminal fop while the categorically white infant grows up to become servile and terrified. Thus, the "slave economy" behind the untroubled, summery downtown of Twain's opening provides the generative energy for *Puddn'head Wilson and Those Extraordinary Twins*. The resolution of that energy—or the unresolved, troubled exposure of it—is provided by the title character.

The enlightened, tinkering rationalist Puddn'head Wilson, Twain's representative in the tale, has the power to reveal the deception of babies switched in the cradle.

Wilson can establish identity with one of his hobbies: the still arcane and mysterious practice of fingerprinting. The loops and whorls on the fingertips of an individual's unique body have a peculiar symbolic relation to the question of nature versus nurture. For one thing, fingerprints can represent the minimal innate difference between two people: in this case, two people on opposite sides of the arbitrary and theoretical, yet lethal, racial divide. The capriciousness of fate, the sexual identity of races, the art of detection, pursued by the scorned man of intellect: these currents, under the placid surface of Dawson's Landing, generate, as well as the nearly incidental murder, an extreme act of betrayal.

Tom sells his mother down the river—that is, he actually *sells* her down the actual southward-flowing *river*, literally, not figuratively. Roxy (though free) is sold by her son, and is sent down the Mississippi to the dreaded cotton plantation country. Roxy and Tom have conspired to keep his secret from discovery. Over-indulged, greedy, and spineless, Tom has accumulated gambling debts. His secret mother, made free by her slave master's will at his death, suggests a solution to Tom's problems. Roxy has no illusions about the young man's sleaziness—nor about his rejection of her, by force of racialist habit—but she means to protect her child. Her solution is grotesque, bizarre, logical, and establishes her moral and intellectual superiority to her offspring:

"I's a nigger," says the apparently white woman to her blue-eyed grown child, "en nobody aint gwyne to doubt it dat hears me talk. I's wuth six hund'd dollars. Take en sell me, en pay off dese gamblers."

As with the opening description of the town, a prolonged passage explodes into terse, capping information at its close: "Tom forged a bill of sale and sold his mother to an Arkansas cotton-planter for a trifle over six hundred dollars." The word "trifle," like Roxy's "nobody . . . dat hears me talk," is a brilliant, sardonic stroke. Roxy is fatally innocent in one regard, resourceful though she is. She supposes that Tom will sell her to someone in town, or in some town, but he betrays her down the river, to the dreaded cotton fields. Ancillary to this, Tom forges the document that makes this free woman his property.

Twain allows us readers to assume that Tom's father was the slave master who in his will made Roxy free. That speculation or likelihood adds a desperate psychological complexity to Tom's forging of a document that dooms his mother and undoes the work—the legally legitimate, if morally craven work—of his father. In another complexity, selling Roxy down the Mississippi also expels her from Dawson's Landing, so that Tom's criminal action, besides abrogating the paternal will also enacts the communal will. The surface peace of Dawson's Landing has been maintained.

Mark Twain clearly had difficulty governing these volatile materials. Entangled with the Puddn'head Wilson story of the switched babies is Twain's farcical narrative of the Siamese twins or two-headed man. The writer put the two stories together and pulled them apart repeatedly, in various published and unpublished formats. He could never separate the stories: the image of two heads with one blood reflected the racial divide in a way that was powerfully true, intricately absurd, and protectively subterranean. On some level that Twain never incorporated into his fiction, the black and white babies are twins. The farce of the Siamese twins Luigi and Angelo—one twin or head drinks, the other is a teetotaler forced to get drunk by their shared blood; one twin is a freethinker, the other is a Methodist—is also an allegory about false innocence and heartless duplicity: in Dawson's Landing, and in the American antebellum slavery-based society that the town of Dawson's Landing, with its peaceful Main Street, represents.

The town's citizen-yokels, who call Wilson "Puddn'head" because they cannot understand irony, set out to hang the guilty twin Luigi at the end of *Those Extraordinary Twins*. Twain dryly portrays the lynching with a noncommittal, even bland surface: a laconic moralist leaving outrage to his reader. In his neutral telling, the community speaks, plurally, as "the people":

> But at last the people came to their senses, and said—
> "Puddn'head was right, at the start—we ought to have hired the official half of that human phillipene to resign, but it's too late, now; some of us haven't got anything left to hire him with."
> "Yes, we have," said another citizen, "we've got this"— and produced a halter.
> Many shouted, "That's the ticket." But others said, "No— Count Angelo is innocent, we mustn't hang him."
> "Who said anything about hanging him? We are only going to hang the other one."
> "Then that is all right—there is no objection to that."
> So they hanged Luigi. And so ends the history of "Those Extraordinary Twins."

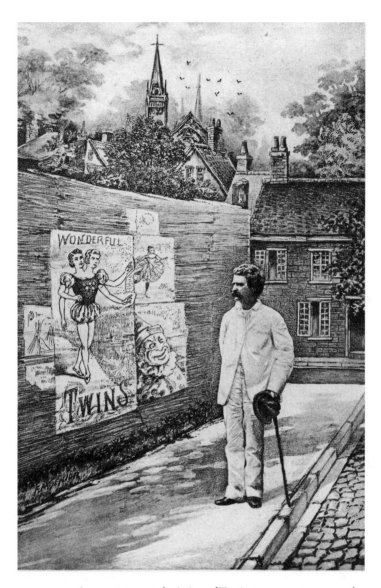

FIGURE 2. A contemporary depiction of Twain on a town street, studying an image of two separate consciousnesses sharing a single blood. Courtesy of Special Collections, University of Virginia Library.

This allegory of blindness, and in particular blindness to how people are related, in this case literally blood to blood, echoes Puddn'head Wilson's defining joke, the joke that when he first came to Dawson's Landing earned him his nickname: wishing he owned half of an annoying, tirelessly barking dog, so that he could kill his half. The townspeople don't get it; it doesn't make sense to them, so they blandly, unanimously brand Wilson as stupid. Twain links Dawson's Landing's isolation of the American intellectual, as embodied by Wilson, with the town's attained unawareness of its own corruption, specifically the race-based abomination of slavery. Twain's characteristic joke on the idea of two halves with one blood, with its lethal point that bewilders the bumpkins who name him "Puddn'head," contains a terrible judgment as well.

II {BROADWAYS}

The English critic William Empson's insight into pastoral is that the need to invent untroubled perfection always springs from anxiety: from suppressed loathing or dread. The dream of ease may be a denial of the nightmare, and therefore by implication a shadowy acknowledgment of it. In a culture notionally built on speed, change, mobility, and expansion, the thought of a quiet, human-scale community has been comforting—a half-real, half-invented shelter, refusing to explode under the successive historical pressures of slavery, economic depression, European war, technological change, imperial enterprises, and global missions, all the violent contradictions of clinging to a complacent provinciality while hurtling forward into the modern, the postmodern, or whatever comes after that.

The American small town recognizable in Twain's account endures in our cultural imagination and, notably, in works of art created during the eighty or ninety years when

13

real towns like it flourished—roughly, the period from Twain's antebellum Dawson's Landing, through the Moonstone of Willa Cather and the Frenchman's Bend of William Faulkner, to the Grover's Corners of Thornton Wilder and the Morgan's Creek of Preston Sturges. (The Oakdale of Sturges's *Hail the Conquering Hero* was literally, though not grammatically, possessed by Woodrow Truesmith's grandfather—the town was the old fellow's farm.)

The possessive form of these place names—with Moonstone a significant exception (though Cather's actual home town contained a "Moon's Buildings")—suggests that the town, like the United States itself, chooses to suppose a recent founding: as though the mill or the landing or the corners or the bend in the river were associated with some specific, actual Frenchman or Grover, Dawson or Morgan who persists in living memory, or who haunts only a little beyond it. Sherwood Anderson leaves off the apostrophe that might follow the name of some founding Wine implicit in his Winesburg, Ohio. The names assert both the nominal survival of a shared history—recent or recently lost—and the brevity, maybe even the shallowness, of that history. The town, in the form of those years of its founding, appeared and faded like a springtime pool.

In the Old World, provinciality might indicate stagnation: the ways and attitudes of petrified villages. Puddn'head Wilson's equivalent in European fictions—the enlightened man of science in Chekhov, Galdós or Ibsen, the progressive doctor or engineer who argues with the village priest—combats a provinciality of the past: the tyranny of precedent, the authority of memory. The corresponding American figure of rationality and progress confronts the opposite: a provinciality rooted in dearth or denial of memory. Twain's pre–Civil War townsmen appeal to no priest or tradition to resist the man of reason Wilson: they meet him, however stupidly, more or less on his own ratiocinative ground. They defend slavery and lynching not by appeal to ancestral ways, but as practices that stand to reason and nourish commerce. Theirs is not the ignorance of inherited shibboleth; it presents itself as though pure, immemorial, and untainted by ancestral prejudice.

Twain and the other makers of these American works are concerned with history and memory, while the communities they depict are not. That disparity supplies a central animation: sometimes explicit as in Faulkner's *The Hamlet,* and sometimes mostly implicit as in Preston Sturges's *The Miracle of Morgan's Creek*—until the political and historical vignettes of that movie's final minutes. The American small town, by now a setting at least half-mythical, provides a mimetic arena where contradictions between slavery and freedom, or between abundance and emptiness, hark back to even more fundamental contradictions: the peculiar anti-intellectual currents within a nation founded as an idea. The town is the imagined locale for American ambivalences about culture itself.

There are still actual towns, of course. Many thousands of them, sometimes prosperous and expanding. But in its heyday the town, though it might seem paradoxical to say so, was central. It was central figuratively, in that its downtown could seem at the core of national economy, culture, politics. More literally, the small town was a center for the surrounding rural countryside. That surrounding and economically antecedent realm, the expanses of territory punctuated by outpost farm, ranch, or camp, precedes the recent founding implicit in those folksy, personalized, and elegiac place names inherited from the murky and transitory Dawson, Grover, Morgan, and Wine: putative individuals reduced to syllables of a nearly perfect yet unsettled forgetting.

In retrospect, from the present, we tend to distinguish the small town from suburb or city; but on the evidence of the movies, and of writers like Twain, Faulkner, and Cather, the primary distinction often was between the town and its country environs. The town was at the center of a surrounding rural life of agriculture or livestock or mining or lumbering that created and sustained the commercial center: a center that in return the countryside relied on, however uneasily, as a storehouse of meanings, practical and social. In that central arena, American artists could trace conflicts between vague, impassioned aspirations toward something lofty, on one side—and on the other, an anti-historical, orphaned, and tormented populism.

The town in that era of its centrality encompassed not only essential social dramas, but the audience for those dramas as well. Book publishers, broadcasters, and movie producers thought about the town, and sought its trade attentively, sometimes obsequiously. Businesses like those and many others—along with statewide and national politicians—courted the small town's defining component, its commons, the avenue of commerce, amusement, and conversation: in the trite, enduring metonymy, "Main Street."

Main Street, like School Street and Church Street, remains a familiar name. All three designations still appear on small-town street signs in every region of the United States. What's more, often those names are still descriptive; unlike the long-gone references of Elm and Grove, a church is probably visible on Church Street and a school, or at least a recognizable converted school building, on School Street.

The thoroughfare and marketplace of Main Street, or Broadway—as it is called in Long Branch, where I was born and raised—has had a more complicated history than Church and School. In a much-noted pattern, the old commercial center is often dead or decayed. The decline of that secular and accessible downtown agora may be regrettable, or not. But it once was, and no longer is, *main*—a principal American locale, in art as well as life. The center of town—where people bought food, clothing, furniture, and hardware, or gathered in theaters, haircutting parlors, bars, coffee shops, and restaurants, or met in halls of the Grange, Elks, Mason, Odd Fellows, or Kiwanis—was for decades a main scene in movies, plays, novels, and poems. From the evidence of these works, the small-town marketplace provided a communal center: more universal than any church, and more significant in daily life than any school.

The towns still exist as cultural, as well as legal and political, entities; but Main and Broadway are no longer as central to a community's vision of itself as the institutions located on School and Church. Those two categories, education and religion, now are main. Religion and education on a local scale provide the unifying or divisive terrain, the common grounds of struggle and recognition—not the old Main Street with its shops, eateries, entertainments, courthouse. Main is no longer main in the sense that it was. The alternate name, "Broadway," with its connotations of grand scale and sophistication, calls up the old, supplanted, and vanished power of that central street, in its thousands of embodiments.

Grief for the loss or diminishment of that thriving downtown may be as pointless as applause for the new electronic cultural core, or for the retail life now strung along the highways. The contemporary movement to revitalize downtowns may be a good thing or not, and it may succeed or not, but it cannot replicate the past. My subject here is the American town as it lives in a few specific, impressive works of art. The meanings in these works are more urgent, more commanding, and more haunted than mere nostalgia.

The town, or its look, still provides the setting of new television dramas, movies, novels. Its emblems and surfaces are aped by architects and developers of shopping malls, amusement parks, residential real estate projects. Franchise chains invoke its imagery with the nostalgia that is a symptom of death, a wan retrospective smile that itself demonstrates how the town these works share, and that I remember, is going or gone.

Main Street with its family-owned shoe store, grocery store, luncheonette, its generations of families that shop and work along that retail spine of a community where they go to school, court, raise new families, and grow old has become increasingly mythical—with all the underground faults and earthshaking, suspended energies of myth. That more or less bygone reality continues as a spectral epitome of the United States itself. Yearning and exasperation, patriotism and derision, love and loathing toward the country and its ways all find expression still in the reassuring idyll or mean hell of Main Street: the miniature agora of a generous American innocence or a nasty, grasping American provincialism or—most characteristically—all of the above.

American fictions have engaged that scene of comforts and pressures: writings and films created when a significant part of their audience lived in small towns. Mark Twain wrote his books in a time when reading provided a principal form of entertainment, with books and newspapers available even in far-flung provinces that lacked theaters or concert halls, lacked even an Elks Hall or any public space larger than chapel or saloon. Willa Cather was a magazine editor by profession, and when she grew up in Red Cloud, Nebraska, reading—as symbolized by a *Collected Works of Balzac*—was a vital means of diversion and information. Preston Sturges and Alfred Hitchcock created their movies when most people in town went to the movies, more or less weekly. In Sturges's *The Miracle of Morgan's Creek,* while the heroine is getting pregnant and wrecking his car, the hero spends all night sitting in front of the movie theater where—in the fib she told her father—they were supposed to have been seeing a show together: a theater exactly like the movie houses where Sturges's audience would be watching his characters.

III {LONG BRANCH}

In my own town, Long Branch, "A" movies played at the *Paramount* (originally the *Broadway*) with its Moorish lobby and golden marquee, its proscenium with large, busty caryatids for columns, its coffered and gilded ceiling. Directly across Broadway was the plainer, streamlined marquee of the *Strand*—its brisk, relatively utilitarian art deco design exciting in its own way—venue for "B" pictures and cowboy matinees. Both theaters had balconies as well as orchestra sections, and just behind the orchestra a part-wall a few feet high, to mark off an area for Standing Room Only. Even the Strand had uniformed ushers. The theaters were owned not by a national chain or corporation, but by a Jersey Shore movie-house magnate. The Paramount today is a shuttered, near-derelict building, used as storage space for a paint business. Developers, it is said, plan to convert the old downtown to a shopping mall, and when they do, the Paramount will

FIGURE 3. Winslow Homer, *The Beach at Long Branch* (1869). Wood engraving on paper (1955.4351). One of Winslow Homer's many depictions of Long Branch. The young woman in the foreground has inscribed the artist's initials in the sand. In the background to the left are the businesses where North Broadway and South Broadway meet Ocean Avenue. © Sterling and Francine Clark Art Institute, Williamstown, Massachusetts.

be restored for live musical shows and concerts. In the idiom of our new century, it will be called the Broadway Art Center.

All four of my grandparents came to live in Long Branch, New Jersey, when they were young. Possibly, the town's glamorous reputation could have been part of the attraction. Long Branch is an ocean resort, a watering spot depicted by Winslow Homer. It was visited by Abraham Lincoln and Diamond Jim Brady: "the Newport of its day." Ulysses Grant relished it as a place for unbuttoned pleasure, for dancing and horse riding. Lingering for weeks after he was struck by an assassin's bullet, President James Garfield was brought from the White House, and the sweltering summer of Washington, to the ocean breezes of Long Branch.

When I grew up there, the beach was eroded, the boardwalk on the famous bluffs given over to honky-tonk, many of the immense Victorian cottages on Ocean Avenue converted to hotels or to "cook-alones": a Yiddish phrase perfectly spelled by the name of the Irish hero Cuchulain. Some of those thirty-room cottages were gutted by Jewish Lightning, as the casual stereotyping of that time and place called arson for insurance money. But when I was growing up in Long Branch, many remained, with their terraced gardens, spandreled galleries, shingled turrets and oriels—now nearly all replaced by apartment complexes.

There were other traces of history: both Grant and Garfield attended services at the Church of the Presidents, as did Chester A. Arthur, Rutherford B. Hayes, Benjamin Harrison, William McKinley and Woodrow Wilson. When the church was dedicated as the Long Branch Historical Museum, I played clarinet in the high school band. An inscribed stone marks the location of the oceanfront cottage where Garfield eventually died—less from the harmlessly encysted bullet fired by Charles Julius Guiteau than from the germs carried by the poking, unwashed fingers of innumerable doctors eager to treat the President. On my way to the Garfield School, I passed the Phil Daly Ladder and Hose, endowed by the celebrated gambler the way other men endowed schools and colleges.

On Broadway my grandfather Morris Eisenberg washed the windows of stores with squeegee and bucket. And on

Broadway my other grandfather kept his bar, the Broadway Tavern. I was eleven or twelve years old before I realized that "Give My Regards to Broadway" was not about our street but one of the same name in Manhattan. In a similar way, when people sighed "the town isn't what it was" or spoke of "the old days," I felt little distinction between the period when my father was a basketball star at Long Branch High School and the glory days of the nineteenth century.

My bar-keeping grandfather Dave Pinsky had been a bootlegger during Prohibition: a small-time gangster. My aunt Thelma says—in the fearful and euphemistic spirit that Willa Cather notes as "the terror of tongues" oppressing little towns—"He was in the liquor business, and it happened to be Prohibition." One or two of the family stories from those days involve boats, and the ocean may have had a practical, commercial importance to Dave. But it is not easy to picture Dave with the spray in his face, or even with his clothes wet: a figure from *The Roaring Twenties,* not *Man of Aran.* He boxed professionally for a time; in photographs he is lounging in a tilted-back chair or scowling and putting up his fists in the traditional pose. He came to Long Branch from Brooklyn, where he was born.

At his Broadway Tavern, across the street from City Hall, politicians and cops came to drink. Local stories were told. During July and August racing season at Monmouth Park, horses were discussed. The characters played by Akim Tamiroff and Brian Donleavy in Sturges's movies would have recognized the place and felt at home there. Knowing that the Chief of Police was a man who worked for my grandfather in the rum-running days gave me a certain pleasurable assurance, along with an insider's sense

FIGURE 4. Dave Pinsky on Broadway in Long Branch, New Jersey, in the 1920s. In an old family joke, the sign says "Paint Store," but it is really a Pint Store.

that in a community things are not always what they seem—that places and people have significant, invisible histories.

The fall from respectability of the town constable played by William Demarest in *The Miracle of Morgan's Creek* seems to me not only plausible but familiar, haloed by old anxieties. Town politicians fire the constable—officially augmenting shame and ostracism with loss of livelihood—after his unmarried daughter becomes pregnant. My father's employer, the optometrist Dr. Alexander Vineburg, a fearsome figure to me, was also for a time the Mayor of Long Branch. Less dramatically than the town elders of Morgan's Creek, Vineburg did eventually fire my father— "let him go" in the euphemism implying permission or a relaxed grasp—not for impropriety or scandal but because, Mayor Vineburg said, it seemed politically advisable, even patriotic, to hire a returning veteran to replace my father. (Milford Pinsky had not served in the military.)

Such small-town calamities and fears, in Long Branch as in Morgan's Creek or Dawson's Landing, might find their counterweight in little marks of a small-town assurance. "Pinsky" was a Long Branch name, thanks in part to the bar—thanks, also, to my father's athletic ability: he and my mother both attended Long Branch High School as did my aunts and uncles, my cousins, my brother, and my sister.

A powerful teacher, like the legendary, demanding English teacher Miss Davis, affected generations in the town. Mailman and lawyer had parsed sentences under Miss Davis's command—"*She'll* make you work," adults used to tell me. She retired before I got to high school, but I did have the same homeroom teacher as my father—the gentler Miss Scott, as though she always got that part of the alphabet. Like the police chief, Miss Scott and Miss Davis contributed to a reassuring fabric that included the bar and sports.

I can hear my father's voice asking me, about an encounter with a teacher, storekeeper, cop, doctor: "Did he know who you were?"

He put this question in a tone not of arrogance, still less of snobbery, but almost the opposite: a kind of egalitarian, citizen's respect for the fabric of the town and its families, the fabric more important than the mere personality of anyone, my father himself or his son or any interlocutor. "Did he know who you were?"—meaning, not how elevated you are, but how interwoven. The other side of the question was information, something like: "I know who he is; his uncles lay asphalt. His grandmother sold her beauty parlor to the Dlugo family. He used to do a specialty number at dance marathons. They had a cousin everybody called Punchy. His brother became a priest." The mingling of place, family, and identity recalls the Homeric question, with its anthropological taproot: "Who are you? Who are your parents, and where do you come from?"

The community spirit, that sense of belonging in a place or being of it, is not loveable in all manifestations. It can be an excuse or channel for anything. A vivid early memory is of a football game between the Green Wave of Long Branch and our enemies, the Asbury Park team—the Blue Bishops. Afterwards, walking across the field holding my uncle's hand, we saw an Asbury Park player, separated from his team, being cursed and threatened by a stocky, flushed Long Branch man—drunk, I now realize. The detailed, obscene threats may have had little denotation for me, but a child could recognize the Asbury Park player's terror and isolation in his blue uniform, the bully's righteous ecstasy, the postgame crowd's aroused anticipation of violence. Without approving of the fat drunk, or feeling complicity with him, a timid child might feel relief at being affiliated with him. Better to be a part of the home town crowd, rather than that menaced outsider.

This vivid, isolated memory may be melodramatic or misleading. The actual sustained playing-out of small-town life for any individual will be diminishing or enabling—almost certainly both at once—at a more inward and intimate level of social identity. And though an American town can seem stable, or even stagnant, a person's or family's identity within it may be thin or transitory. The stories are immigrant stories, one way or another. To say that Pinsky was a Long Branch name reaches back a mere three generations, to my grandparents. Because so many of our family went through the schools, and because of the bar, we could seem and feel part of the place's fabric, within four or five decades. As with the elegiac blanks of "Frenchman's Bend" and "Grover's Corners," the point of such history may be less its depth than its newness, its short-lived quality: within living memory, or nearly so. Forgetting demonstrates the passage and immensity of time, in a way tradition cannot.

There is a difference between history and lore, parallel to the differences between education and experience, or learning and cunning. Lore is a form of transmitted memory not only more provincial than history, but more homey. It has a peasant or burgher quality: shrewd rather than epic or heroic, and unlike the scholarly chronicles of history, the recounting of lore is quite ready to draw practical or moral instruction from its materials. If history incorporates each little place into larger patterns or forces, lore allegorizes the place itself.

Long Branch lore, in my days there, included celebrated children of families with retail businesses on Broadway, in particular the Jewish shopkeepers. One of those little stores—was it paint and hardware?—belonged to the parents of the great literary scholar M. H. Abrams. Another mom-and-pop business paid for the first lessons of the noted pianist Julius Katchen. The parents of Jeff Chandler, the movie star who played Cochise in *Broken Arrow,* owned a delicatessen; their name was Grossel. Norman Mailer's aunt had a dress shop. (Mailer's grandfather was a Long Branch rabbi.)

An eminent junkyard in Long Branch used to belong to a man called, oddly enough, Ash. He was a contemporary of Meyer Abrams—"Mike Abrams" in town—and of my father. Izzy Ash knew my father as a certain kind of high school boy: voted "Best-Looking Boy" by his graduating class from Long Branch High School and a star athlete on a successful team called "The Jewish Aces." I went to Izzy Ash's junkyard in the summer of 1962 to get a part for a 1953 Dodge convertible that I proposed to drive out to California. I intended to be a poet, and with that goal I was going to Stanford. Mr. Ash took this in as he grunted and tugged at a long-handled wrench, removing the part I needed from a wrecked Coronet.

I told Mr. Ash that I was going to graduate school, not that I was going to be a writer. As it happened, he knew more than might be expected about going to graduate school. And I had already, that summer, been embarrassed by the idea that I was a writer.

FIGURE 5. The Jewish Aces posing for a group portrait on the steps of Long Branch High School in 1939, with Milford Pinsky holding the trophy.

A Long Branch boy named Danny Pingitore had been having some minor success under another name as a television actor. The absurdity that comes with ambitions like those each of us had planned to take West came up when Danny phoned me earlier that summer. Like the Sturges characters played by Eddie Bracken, I seemed to have become an inadvertent liar, helpless between a communal gaze that apparently knew me well and my own ill-formed, vulnerable idea of who I might actually be.

I didn't exactly know Danny, he was at least five years older than me, but our two families knew one another. Our mothers had run into one another in a store, and Danny was back in Long Branch for a couple of weeks in July.

"Robert, this is Danny Pingitore. Your mother says you're heading out to California, to be a writer?"

"Well, yes."

"There's something I really want to tell you."

"What's that?"

"Don't go."

"What?"

"Don't go, Robert, I mean it. I know a lot of writers in L.A. and they all say this is the worst year for it. Things were okay, but now they aren't producing any more hour shows at all. Everything is half-hour shows. Half-hour is all they're making—and most of the writers out there already can't get work. Hour shows are dead."

So I told Mr. Ash only that I was going to Stanford, to graduate school. In Izzy Ash's class at Long Branch High School there were two outstanding students, both from Jewish families. Both went to Harvard: Mike Abrams and Barry Green, two brilliant and ambitious Long Branch boys whose stories still meant something to Mr. Ash as he braced his feet against the sandy, shadeless, oil-stained earth of his junkyard and pulled a part free along its channeled bracket. He had his generation's respect for what doing well in school could do for one whose family had no money or power. So he told me the story of Mike and Barry.

Mike Abrams went from Harvard College to graduate school and became a distinguished professor, the author of a famous book. (This was *The Mirror and the Lamp*, a study of the two central Romantic images for poetry. I had not exactly read this work of scholarship, but I knew by authority that it was very good; and so it did turn out to be.) Barry Green also had a brain that propelled him over the anti-Semitic barriers erected by Harvard—barriers that young Jews of that era practically embraced, because like Goliath the barriers increased the glory of overcoming them. Barry went on to become a rich, clever lawyer, but sadly—as Mr. Ash told me the story he knew I knew—in the course of his climb to success Barry Green got himself in deep with the Mob, with secret arrangements and fixings including a deal that involved selling orange peels to the government, supposedly for the production of synthetic sugar. The deal was saturated in fraud, bribery, chicanery, and even despoiling of the U.S. Treasury in wartime.

The dukes and generals of the Mob maintained a long-standing base in Long Branch. Protecting the myth of their patriotism, they declared that Barry Green would have to go to prison, and so he did. The alternative was testifying, and sudden disappearance. His family—the two daughters, both beautiful, took elocution lessons, and the younger one was the first girl in town to play Little League—were looked after conscientiously and abundantly by those powerful dukes.

Meanwhile, the story concluded, Mike Abrams continued the idyllic life of an honored professor at Cornell University, an Ivy League college hardly less glorious than Harvard itself. Mr. Ash sighed emphatically. Wiping his brow with his forearm, he finished with a moral:

"Yes, Robert, there's two different paths in life: it's just like North Broadway and South Broadway."

Having pronounced this lesson, Izzy Ash held out to me the extracted, rebuildable fuel pump of the Coronet. Broadway's two forks, North and South, form a Y just a couple of blocks from the beach. One of the things that seemed funny to me about Mr. Ash's allegorizing of the town, even as I nodded solemnly, is that North Broadway and South Broadway extended only to arrive at the same destination—the Atlantic Ocean, and Long Branch's boardwalk with its clam shacks, custard stands, and amusement arcades.

The vast ocean, the little streets: in a folk form, the fundamental, however laughable-feeling impulse to allegorize the local and its lore. The tale's themes of heroism and failure, moralism and practicality, its shrewd gossipy relish of both misdeeds and accomplishments, its comic or tragic or melodramatic extremes, reflect the forces that make literature. Jim Burden, the protagonist of Willa Cather's *My Ántonia,* as a student at the State University, mulls Virgil's words in the third book of the "Georgics":

"Primus ego in patriam mecum . . . deducam Musas"; "for I shall be the first, if I live, to bring the Muse into my country." Cleric had explained to us that "patria" here meant, not a nation or even a province, but the little rural neighborhood where the poet was born. This was not a boast, but a hope, at once bold and devoutly humble.

The elevation of small-town streets to heroic fable is a primitive embryo of culture itself. It is also an embryo of the mean, judgmental, unforgiving mentality of the provinces, Cather's "terror of the tongues."

In Mr. Ash's Long Branch narrative, the distinctively American threads include immigrant ambition (there are Jewish and Chinese shopkeepers downtown even in Faulkner's Jefferson, and a similar immigrant character is the most benign figure in Sturges's *Miracle of Morgan's*

Creek) and an ambivalent awe toward the forces of lawless power: gunslingers or gangsters or—even in the North, even in Long Branch as it turns out, an historical force—Klansmen.

There is a horror to the small-town gaze, its readiness to judge and categorize, its narrowness. Willa Cather and her artist heroine, Thea Kronborg, even more than Twain's Puddn'head Wilson, feel that horror sharply. But on the other hand, the sagacious and cosmopolitan Mr. Ottenburg, foreseeing Thea's accomplishments as an artist, says to her ally, who nods in agreement: "Her scale of values will always be the Moonstone scale. And, with an artist, that is an advantage." And Thea herself will say, after she has attained world recognition: "Nearly all my dreams, except those about breaking down on the stage or missing trains, are about Moonstone."

IV {SIMPLE, ETERNAL PROBLEMS}

The binary, perhaps reductive, division into dream and nightmare has a brilliant epitome in Kenneth Tynan's two-edged parody, "Just Plain Folks." Reviewing a 1957 play based on William Faulkner's *Requiem for a Nun,* Tynan puts a description of Faulkner's town into the mouth of the Stage Manager from Thornton Wilder's play *Our Town.* The British critic Tynan's evocation of the two authors presents a mythology of the American town, folksy and appalling, hyperbolic yet subtle, with the nuance that inspired parody can attain:

> Well, folks, reckon that's about it. End of another day in the city of Jefferson, Yoknapatawpha County, Mississippi. Nothin' much happened. Couple of people got raped, couple more got their teeth kicked in, but way up there those far-away old stars are still doing their old cosmic criss-cross, and there ain't a thing we can do about it. It's pretty quiet

now. Folk hereabouts get to bed early, those that can still walk. Down behind the morgue a few of the young people are roastin' a nigger over an open fire, but I guess every town has its night-owls, and afore long they'll be tucked up asleep like anybody else. Nothin' stirring down at the big old plantation house—you can't even hear the hummin' of that electrified barbed-wire fence, 'cause last night some drunk ran slap into it and fused the whole works. That's where Mr. Faulkner lives, and he's the fellow that thought this whole place up, kind of like God. Mr. Faulkner knows everybody round these parts like the back of his hand, 'n most everybody round these parts knows the back of Mr. Faulkner's hand. But he's not home right now, he's off on a trip round the world as Uncle Sam's culture ambassador, tellin' foreigners about how we've got to love everybody, even niggers, and how integration's bound to happen in a few thousand years anyway, so we might just as well make haste slowly. Ain't a thing we can do about it.

(He takes out his watch and consults it.)

Along about now the good folk of Jefferson City usually get around to screamin' in their sleep. Just ordinary people havin' ordinary nightmares, the way most of us do most of the time.

(An agonized shrieking is briefly heard.)

Ayeah, there they go. Nothin' wrong there that an overdose of Seconal won't fix.

(He pockets his watch.)

Like I say, simple folk fussin' and botherin' over simple, eternal problems.

Here two American provincialities, New England and the Deep South, are evoked and burlesqued in all of their debatable New-ness and Deep-ness. Wilder's New Hampshire and Faulkner's Mississippi in the parody become equivalent, the choice of one or another by implication arbitrary, an absurd decor or idiom, based on extremes of the folksy and the violent. The very notion of a small stage revealing large realities is itself parodied, with our lethal history of racism and our overdose of Seconal bundled complacently with the "old cosmic criss-cross" and the philosophical bumpkin's pocket watch.

Tynan's final, crowning phrases—"simple folk fussin' and botherin' over simple, eternal problems"—suggest an absurdity that inheres not only in Thornton Wilder's Grover's Corners or in William Faulkner's Jefferson, but perhaps—so one might argue—in Homeric Ithaca or Troy or Thebes or Shakespeare's imagined Denmark or ancient Britain. These, too, are local stages for cosmic forces. In principle, Faulkner's rapes and lynchings are no meaner, no less heroic or archetypal, than the murders, adulteries, human sacrifices and betrayals recounted by Homer or Sophocles. But Homer and Sophocles imagine the Olympian immortals as looking on, and even intervening, as mortal rivalries, grudges, ambitions and adulteries take place on some tribally contested beach or plain, or in the bed chambers and encampments of a powerful local household.

The tragic or heroic microcosm is not aware of its smallness: the world of the Achaeans and Trojans, or of the Thebans, is all in all to itself. That world's drama is within itself and its own past. The town, in contrast, identifies itself as a little center away from the larger center; its drama or struggle is precisely with the outside world, and with a past that may not belong to it. Up to a certain age, I did have Long Branch's Broadway mixed up with the New York street of George Cohan's song—an epic-scale innocence. But the adult, ordinary street itself knows that it is one of thousands of Broadways—a provincial's knowledge of provinciality is part of Mr. Ash's pleasure in his allegory, and part of its effect on his audience.

Main Street's narrative includes that dwindling yet in a way comforting perspective of its own interchangeable, provincial and bourgeois nature. The novel and film are consciously middle-class forms; our world of Main Street and Seconal is aware of some larger or older or more important, perhaps even more heroic human world beyond it: perhaps in the great historic capitals of glamour and power. In the storm-torn clouds above Lear's Britain, as beyond the walls of Thebes or the beach at Troy, the only larger realm is that of the observant, often partisan gods.

An attentive parody is a tribute, as well as a debunking. Tynan's wit illuminates the double role of Grover's Corners and Jefferson: places that are ordinary and extreme, small yet quintessential, classic in their fundamental, stark energies though provincially regional in their American manners. They are comic in the scale of their particularity, a distinct but limited quiddity. The Englishman Tynan's parody also establishes in a few quick strokes another much-noted theme: an indomitable American belief in our own innocence, impervious to reality. The folksy character's bland acceptance of rapin' and lynchin' is funny partly because it epitomizes a familiar question of innocence and blindness. Faulkner's speeches about a racial integration that will occur by-and-by, "in a few thousand years anyway," occupy the perceptible apex of a mountainous national hypocrisy,

FIGURE 6. Downtown square of Oxford, Mississippi, William Faulkner's home town. Courtesy of Mississippi Department of Archives and History.

but Tynan implicitly includes Wilder and his microcosm. Is an a-historical provincialism, convinced of its own innocence, the most monstrous kind? At what point do the sources of a familiar backwater pastoral nourish a monstrous complacency?

V {FRENCHMAN'S BEND}

Gabriel Garcia Marquez, in an interview with his American colleague William Kennedy (author of *Ironweed* and other works about his province of Albany and the towns of up-state New York), says that "the best South American novel ever written" is *The Hamlet* by William Faulkner. This statement pleases me immensely, because I have long thought that the best novel ever written about the New Jersey Shore is *The Hamlet* by William Faulkner. In this work, Faulkner sees into the heart of something essential, in the miniature alembic of the partly legendary, half-obsolete, incipient but stubbornly magnetic American town. His novel attains the authority of myth partly because the "hamlet"—the word's Germanic roots mean "little home"—is the smallest possible unit that could be called a town.

The phrase "little town" had a very early poetic power for me. In the Garfield School, at assembly, the high-pitched voices of us primary school students moved me,

soaring high in the Christmas carol with its mysteriously
powerful images:

> O little town of Bethlehem!
>   How still we see thee lie,
> Above thy deep and dreamless sleep,
>   The silent stars go by;
> Yet in thy dark streets shineth
>   The Everlasting light;
> The hopes and fears of all the years
>   Are met in thee tonight.

In Long Branch, with its population that doubled for
a couple of months each summer, the streets each year
felt drained and suddenly quiet when the season ended,
the days getting noticeably shorter, and the lights on the
boardwalk going dark, the honky-tonk music silent. Those
associations would explain some of the song's power.

The hymn "O Little Town of Bethlehem" was written by
Phillips Brooks (1835–1893), a Boston clergyman famous
for his pulpit eloquence on the subject of the Civil War
dead. The stanza that moved me, with its dark streets and
silent stars, includes also Bethlehem's "deep and dreamless sleep," a phrase that in 1868 when Brooks wrote his
lines would evoke towns in the North and South made
unnaturally silent by the absence of so many young men.
In the context of that recent Civil War, "the hopes and
fears of all the years," met in the dark streets, called up the
hopes and fears of the Republic itself.

The implicit memory of the Civil War dead, or something more like an implicit sense of absence, generates the
hymn's cultural power, a shadowed radiance of deep and

dreamless sleep and the silence of dark streets. "O Little Town of Bethlehem" is embedded in American culture with the peculiar depth and pathos of the half-remembered. In my school named for an assassinated President, in a place where the big hotel on Broadway was the Garfield-Grant, possibly there was some additional resonance to Phillips Brooks's words: not in anything that I *knew,* exactly, but in a vague realm of what I might intuit that the town of Long Branch knew. The carol's images gained emotional force from a sense of indistinct, persistent history. If I could not name that history, I might feel that someone in Long Branch knew it, or even if no one in the town knew the history, we shared a collective sense of it, however vague, or even repressed, the communal knowing might be.

Faulkner tells *The Hamlet* partly from a plural, communal point of view. The Faulknerian way of saying "what the town knew" and "the town understood that" or "the town could see" may have inspired some of Garcia Marquez's way of telling stories from the viewpoint of Macondo. Twain's "the people came to their senses" is one of many antecedents. Such telling has been described as "choral," with the idea that as in Greek tragedy we hear the collective or general voice of the community. Thornton Wilder's character the Stage Manager, parodied by Tynan, is a chorus and Faulkner's men whittling on the porch of Varner's store have been called a chorus. Possibly so, but that choral notion—the vocal, corrective, and ordinary norm of Thebes or Athens responding to the sacrifices and excesses of heroes—may neglect the tension, anger, menace, and oppressive insularity of the town as Faulkner portrays it. Faulkner's narrator suggests that the insularity is even temporal as well as spatial, abrogating or invalidating memory—the opposite of a tragic chorus's allusive reminders of the past.

The events of *The Hamlet* follow the classic tale of the intruder—which is an inside-out version of the even older folk story of the successful upstart: the youth from nowhere who becomes King or marries the King's daughter. The intruder story is the lucky-upstart story told from the viewpoint of the old order, rather than the adventuresome hero. The two ways of looking at the story correspond roughly to the province defending itself against what might come from a larger, possibly historical stage and the province taking pride in the mark its children might make on that stage.

In the old order of Frenchman's Bend, an outlying hamlet to the small town of Jefferson, Mississippi, the Varner family holds the sources of power. The Varners' general store, their mortgages on most of the region's farms, and above all their cotton scales, dominate the local economy. The blacksmith is Varner's blacksmith, and the sharecroppers are tenants on Varner soil, in Varner shanties. The sharecropper Ab Snopes gains a foothold by threatening the Varners with his reputation for barn-burning, a threat Ab need not utter because he knows that gossip will deliver it to the target. Gradually, Frenchman's Bend slips from Varner hands into the grip of Ab's son: the shrewd, laconic, apparently soul-less Flem Snopes. Flem outwits even the wily, reflective sewing machine agent Ratliff—the closest Faulkner comes to an authorial representative in the story, as Puddn'head Wilson is in Twain's. That is the nominal or outward story of *The Hamlet*: the Rise of Snopes.

The inner story is darker in all senses, including the dark of moral blindness: the hamlet is aware of Snopes;

but in a way that recalls Twain's complacent and corrupted town, Frenchman's Bend seems unaware of how much like Snopes it is, and how deeply Snopes reflects the place. He embodies it, and he brings it to its extreme logical extension. The uncertainty or absence of any moral distinction between Snopeses and Varners propels the rise of Flem the intruder, sinister and unattractive though he is. Flem Snopes may be a disruptive force, but the insular community of Frenchman's Bend teems with its own conflicts, violent and savage within itself as well as toward the larger world. Faulkner's narrator describes the population with a peculiar blend of comedy and terror, relish and appall:

Federal officers went into the country and vanished. Some garment which the missing man had worn might be seen—a felt hat, a broadcloth coat, a pair of city shoes or even his pistol—on a child or an old man or woman. County officers did not bother them at all save in the heel of election years. They supported their own churches and schools, they married and committed infrequent adulteries and more frequent homicides among themselves and were their own courts, judges and executioners. They were Protestants and Democrats and prolific; there was not one Negro landowner in the entire section. Strange Negroes would absolutely refuse to pass through it after dark.

The community's relation to the outside world seems minimal: they vote, and they kill Federal officers. These comic stereotypes of rural Southern whites are not, strictly speaking, anonymous: they have names "from the Scottish and Welsh Marches": ". . . Turpin and Haley and

45

Whittington, McCallum and Murray . . . and other names like Riddup and Armistid and Doshey which could have come from nowhere since certainly no man would deliberately select one of them for his own."

Isolated by geography from the larger world they seem isolated from historical time as well, without history or perhaps even the idea of history, no contortion or elegance of the past whatsoever: "They brought no slaves and no Phyfe and Chippendale highboys." Removed as they are in time as well as space, unfed by any temporal stream of future aspiration or historical knowledge, the inhabitants of Frenchman's Bend cannot always distinguish time from space: they refer to the plantation builder whose ruined mansion they strip for firewood as "The Old Frenchman," since to them "anyone speaking the tongue with a foreign flavor or whose appearance or even occupation was strange, would have been a Frenchman regardless of what nationality he might affirm, just as to their more urban coevals (if he had elected to settle in Jefferson itself, say) he would have been called a Dutchman." Unlike Dawson or Grover, Faulkner's Frenchman is forgotten even as a name, even as people called Riddup and Doshey have forgotten their original names: Faulkner imagines a community that paradoxically, while bound by the old traditional plantation hierarchies of race and property, also approaches an apparent extreme of forgetting. The proto-downtown of Varner's store is as close as the community comes to a civic space.

Here at the outset of *The Hamlet,* only the urbane, scornful yet fascinated voice that tells this a-historical history seems aware of any larger frame. Only the narrative itself harks back to the world of Phyfe and Chippendale

FIGURE 7. A scene from the 1949 film version of Faulkner's *Intruder in the Dust*. Courtesy of MGM/Photofest, Inc.

and the Middle Passage, a slavery economy and by implication the Civil War and Reconstruction. In political or social space, so in social time, a minimal civilization approaches or seems to approach the absolute zero of complete freedom from the past, just as it approaches the absolute zero of freedom from government. The hamlet of Frenchman's Bend appears to live in the unpunctuated monotony of its own dreamy though violent present tense. The menacing timelessness of Frenchman's Bend suggests the obverse of the pastoral calm that introduces Dawson's Landing.

The force that comes from outside to dispel that illusion, the Snopes family, actually embodies the characteristics of the community—can even be said to epitomize the community, in an extreme, concentrated form: indifferent to their own irrelevant origins, impoverished, suspicious, independent, scornful of social arrangements, reliant entirely on their own greed and cunning. The desperate sharecropper Mink Snopes commits murder; the idiot Ike Snopes violates sexual mores by falling in love, and tenderly coupling, with a cow; I. O. Snopes with his astonishing, habitual, meaning-refuting manner of speech, consistently violates, by easeful and unself-consciously cynical abuse, the very nature of human discourse itself, as when he utters the memorable sentence, regarding Ike and the cow:

> The Snopes name has done held its head up too long in this country to have no such reproaches against it like stock-diddling.

Incidental to this outrageous, parodic declaration of provincial respectability, I. O. arrogates for his family of definitive interlopers the status of old inhabitants. (Persistent rumor in Faulkner's home town of Oxford, Mississippi, alleges that the Snopeses are identifiably and vengefully modeled on a particular, actual family that consider themselves to be old Southern gentry.)

And the Snopeses do fit the narrator's description of the community: if names like Riddup and Doshey seem to Faulkner or his persona something "no man would deliberately select . . . for his own," surely that goes double for the rodent-like, insinuating sound, "Snopes." As a force within Faulkner's microcosm, the Snopes family raises the perhaps especially American question: in the theoretical absence of acknowledged historical memory, how can anyone be considered an interloper? Flem Snopes in this way embodies William Faulkner's despair at the communal action of ignoring or failing to acknowledge its history.

Faulkner's comic relish and anguished disgust together comprise a recognizable attitude toward the town: the ambivalence of an artist who records its general stupidities and treasures its unexpected gallantries, who esteems the particular community as a grail of memories and epitomes, and who loathes its willful isolation, its populist anti-intellectualism. The authorial figure—the unconventional Westerner Willa Cather with her town of Moonstone, the Southerner Twain with his Dawson's Landing, the cosmopolitan Preston Sturges with his mythical Morgan's Creek—finds in the town's absences (absence of the past, absence of imagination, absence of connection to anything larger) the fascination of a microcosm and the claustrophobia of an island. The outsider who intrudes to set things going operates as the artist's agent—or possibly more, the artist's covert alter ego, however villainous.

In Frenchman's Bend, the intruder Flem Snopes resembles Faulkner in at least the two qualities of ambition and detachment. The italicized, hyperbolic parable of Flem and Satan can be seen, in this respect, as an authorial fantasy of power or triumph. The passage simultaneously scorns and glorifies the locale and its idiom and its representative man Flem—scorns and glorifies the place partly by exaggerating the depths of Flem's evil:

> . . . *baffled, they come to the Prince his self.*
> '*Sire,*' *they says,* '*he just won't. We can't do nothing with him.*'
> '*What?*' *the Prince hollers.*

49

'He says a bargain is a bargain. That he swapped in good faith and honor, and now he has come to redeem it, like the law says. And we can't find it, they says. 'We done looked everywhere. It wasn't no big one to begin with nohow, and we was specially careful in handling it. . . . but when we opened the compartment, it was gone. . . . and the seal wasn't broke. But there wasn't nothing in the matchbox but a little kind of dried-up smear under one edge. . . . how can we redeem him into eternal torment without his soul?

The dialect and the hyperbole have the tremendous verve of comic vengeance, and Faulkner lets the scene gather detail until—like so much in his work, and so much in town life—everything comes down to a business transaction:

> *'I come about that soul,' he says.*
> *'So they tell me,' the Prince says. 'But you have no soul.'*
> *'Is that my fault?' he says.*
> *'Is it mine?' the Prince says. 'Do you think I created you?'*
> *'Then who did?' he says. And he had the Prince there.*

And eventually the Prince of Darkness falls scrabbling and screaming to the hot floor while Flem, straw suitcase in hand, waits calmly for his due. "Like I say," as Thornton Wilder's *Our Town* Stage Manager says in Kenneth Tynan's parody: "simple folk fussin' and botherin' over simple, eternal problems."

VI {SHADOWS OF DOUBT}

The comic vibration between "simple" and "eternal" is also a gulf, with a component of rage at a folksy simplicity in love with itself. As with Twain's dialect, the regional speech is both relished and turned against itself. In a more neutral, cosmopolitan idiom, the emotion turned against the complacent townsfolk is shocking in another way. Here is an evocation of that rage, also invoking Hell, and also explicitly invoking blindness—in a setting more naturalistic than Faulkner's, in a monologue nasty with actual, paranoiac menace—but also with its detectable undertone of comic hyperbole:

You think you know something, don't you? You think you're the clever little girl who knows something. There's so much you don't know. So much. What do you know, really? You're just an ordinary little girl in an ordinary little town. You wake up every morning of your life and you know perfectly well that there's nothing in the world to trouble you. You go through your ordinary little day and at night you sleep your untroubled, ordinary little sleep filled with peaceful, stupid dreams. And I brought you nightmares . . . or did I? Was it a silly, inexpert little lie? You're a sleepwalker—blind! How do you know what the world is like? Do you know the world is a foul sty? Do you know if you ripped the fronts off houses, you'd find swine? The world's a hell; what does it matter what happens in it?

This speech is from *Shadow of a Doubt,* the movie Alfred Hitchcock identified as his favorite among his own works. I quote the passage because Hitchcock's film is a marvelous American work of art about nightmare concealing itself in an American town—and because the screenwriter is Thornton Wilder.

In Hitchcock's film the character who utters these words is a charming, handsome and well-dressed serial killer named Charlie. He addresses his lecture to a young woman, his niece named after him, also called Charlie. This "the world's a hell" speech is delivered while the two Charlies, uncle and niece, played by Joseph Cotten and Teresa Wright, are sitting in a surprisingly low, film noir-ish bar in the mostly wholesome town of Santa Rosa, California. (In a touch that reminds me of Long Branch, the spacey, vaguely sinister waitress went to high school with Charlie-the-ingénue.) At the movie's outset, before her mother's disturbing but good-looking brother has come to visit, young Charlie complains to her father that their lives are too ordinary and dull.

That sentiment—however questionable in the light of serial murder and the young woman's mortal danger—

FIGURE 8. "Do you know if you ripped the fronts off houses, you'd find swine?" Joseph Cotten as a gregarious, dapper serial killer and Patricia Collinge as his adoring sister in Alfred Hitchcock's *Shadow of a Doubt*. Courtesy of Universal Pictures/Photofest, Inc.

confirms what the movie shows us of Santa Rosa, a place innocuous and ordinary-looking enough to recall the complacent, nearly immobile Main Street of Twain's slave-owning town. By speaking of the foul sty or hell of the world, specifically of the foul world behind the facades of houses, the handsome, dapper killer played by Joseph Cotten speaks for Wilder and Hitchcock as well: the young girl does indeed underestimate the depths of corruption in the world, as she comes painfully to realize eventually, while her family and fellow citizens continue to sleepwalk.

That sleepwalking or oblivious quality is the point of the Stage Manager's actual, concluding speech in *Our Town*—the passage so brilliantly parodied by Kenneth Tynan:

FIGURE 9. From the 1940 film version of *Our Town,* which was shot in Fort Bragg, California. The lane, with its evocative series of fences, entrances, overlooking windows, and the street and fence in the background, suits Wilder's sense of a town's mysteries, charm, and claustrophobia. Courtesy of United Artists/Photofest, Inc.

Most everybody's asleep in Grover's Corners. There are a few lights on: Shorty Hawkins, down at the depot, has just watched the Albany train go by. And at the Livery stable somebody's setting up late and talking.—Yes, it's clearing up. There are the stars—doing their old, old crisscross journeys in the sky. Scholars haven't settled the matter yet, but they seem to think there are no living beings up there. Just chalk . . . or fire. Only this one is straining away, straining away all the time to make something of itself. The strain's so bad that every sixteen hours everybody lies down and gets a rest.

Then the stage direction says: "*He winds his watch.*"

The watch, like the stars of chalk or fire, represents Wilder's preoccupation with mortality, the vastness of time, and the brevity of life. His play inquires, under the heading of eternity, into the meaning of specific ordinary lives, in a particular if interchangeable or generic place. Act III takes place in the Grover's Corners cemetery, where the dead, including characters we have seen alive at the play's outset, speak as part of their "weaning from the earth."

And among those dead, too, as in Wilder's screenplay for the Hitchcock film, an angry male character scolds a young woman—he acerbic and she innocent even in her regretful disillusion, though both of them are dead. Emily Gibbs, who has died young in childbirth, laments that she lived without noticing she was alive. "That's all human beings are!" says Emily, "Just blind people."

Then the suicide choir master Simon Stimson says to her, from his grave:

Yes, now you know. Now you know! That's what it was to be alive. To move about in a cloud of ignorance; to go up and down trampling on the feelings of those . . . of those about you. To spend and waste time as though you had a million years. To be always at the mercy of one self-centered passion, or another. Now you know—that's the happy existence you wanted to go back to. Ignorance and blindness.

The refutation of these dark words, their contradiction by the benign Mrs. Gibbs, is qualified: "Simon Stimson, that ain't the whole truth and you know it." Then Mrs. Gibbs alludes to the symbols of eternity, chalk or fire: "Emily, look at that star. I forget its name."

This cosmic-scale, posthumous debate includes the setting of what the Hitchcock murderer calls ordinary lives in the hell of an ordinary little place. When George, a living character, falls down sobbing on Emily's grave, a couple of dead women comment with village obtuseness, as amiable and unseeing as Twain's lynching party: "Goodness! That ain't no way to behave!" And "He ought to be home!" And then, as a comment on those ordinary, banal village cluckings, and on all of Grover's Corners, comes the last exchange, just before that summarizing speech used so cleverly by Tynan. The exchange is between Emily and Mrs. Gibbs:

> "Mother Gibbs?"
> "Yes, Emily?"
> "They don't understand, do they?"
> "No, dear. They don't understand."

This teasing valedictory passage expresses both a measure of tenderness toward the townspeople and certainty that they are in some essential way entirely, blindly unaware.

Unknowing is part of the town's meaning: in its oblivion (or obliviousness) it supplies both the comfort of being known and an alienating ignorance or emptiness. The tradition of voices speaking from the grave, to summarize particular lives or life in general, reaches back to the epitaphs of the Greek Anthology, through Wilder's more immediate predecessor Edgar Lee Masters. His popular *Spoon River Anthology* consists of lyric poems spoken from the grave by an assortment of types: adulterous wife, penny-pinching shopkeeper, roughneck, snob, drunkard. "Minerva Jones" begins:

I am Minerva, the village poetess,
Hooted at, jeered at, by the Yahoos of the street
For my heavy body, cock-eye and rolling walk,
And all the more when "Butch" Weldy
Captured me after a brutal hunt.

One of Masters's least sympathetic characters, Archibald
Higbie, got out of town, though he is buried there:

I loathed you, Spoon River, I tried to rise above you,
I was ashamed of you, I despised you
As the place of my nativity.
And there in Rome, among the artists,
Speaking Italian, speaking French,
I seemed to myself at times to be free
Of every trace of my origin.

Masters is not a subtle writer. These opening lines seem
to foreshadow a change of heart or reversal of some kind,
but the character's last words are similar to his first:

There was no culture, you know, in Spoon River,
And I burned with shame and held my peace.
And what could I do, all covered over
And weighted down with western soil,
Except aspire, and pay for another
Birth in the world, with all of Spoon River
Rooted out of my soul?

There's deliberate as well as inadvertent comedy in the
testy, heavy-handed speeches that Masters puts into the
mouths of his posthumous speakers. And as with *Our*

FIGURE 10. Thornton Wilder and Alfred Hitchcock surveying the center of Santa Rosa, California. The location for *Shadow of a Doubt* strikingly resembles the set used by Preston Sturges for both *The Miracle of Morgan's Creek* and *Hail the Conquering Hero*. Photographer: J. R. Eyerman. Courtesy of Time & Life Pictures/Getty Images.

Town in its more elegantly fluent mode, the Spoon River voices thirst for some overarching, metaphysical context for their backwater situation. The "village poetess" Minerva Jones ends her lyric complaint with a blatant, desperate, emphatic plea: "Will someone go to the village newspaper, / And gather into a book the verses I wrote?— / I thirsted so for love! / I thirsted so for life!"

Thornton Wilder brings a subtler, more cosmopolitan sensibility to the methods and materials of Masters's sequence of poems. An Ivy Leaguer who had lived in Wisconsin, California, New England, New Jersey, Wilder makes his focus not thwarted desires for love or art but a cosmic unknowing, a misapprehension of the universe, his characters' unawareness of eternity. Twain concentrates on an immediate functional stupidity of Dawson's Landing: a moral quality more repellent and calamitous than mere lack of intelligence. I imagine he would laugh at Masters's line, "There was no culture, you know, in Spoon River," as well as understanding it—as would Faulkner, whose subject is in part the extinction of culture, history, nobility—the arid, materialist residue of Flem Snopes's victory. The European Hitchcock (*Shadow of a Doubt,* released in 1943, was made when the director was a still a newcomer to California, with World War II in progress) seems interested in his new country's strange combination of sleepwalking shallowness and its resilient—or its superficial?—decency. Willa Cather's work is more heated than all of these; and the films of Preston Sturges are more cool.

VII {MORGAN'S CREEK}

The town can seem benignly welcoming, but its embrace can also suffocate, or turn nasty and punitive. It can kill with a brutality all the more terrible because it is unaware. The citizens of the town recognize one another: they know one another extensively or even intimately, though without perceiving the nature of a psychopathic killer like Joseph Cotten's Uncle Charlie or an intelligence like Puddn'head Wilson's. That imperfect but extended communal knowledge presents a tantalizing palliative for the anonymity and alienation of modern life. Or, that same communal knowledge becomes an alienation that is more punishing because of its generating intimacy: a viciously judgmental provinciality. It can concentrate something like the terrible blood-force of family rejection. In another knot of contradictory energies, the town does after all possess a genuine if unacknowledged or ignored history, harking back to the Indians of Faulkner's South or

Cather's Midwest, and it can also seem static and eternal. It may be touched by great wars overseas, but it responds to them in its own terms.

The contrast or merging of high and low, perceptive and blind, familiar and alien—in a more manic and rapid way—is part of Preston Sturges's art, too. Sturges's characters speak allusively, poetically, or with sophisticated wit; and on the other hand, they also execute amazing pratfalls, slapstick fights. In his audacious screenplays and in his directing style, Sturges establishes a right to shift rapidly among modes and moods, careening with an urbane, manic freedom from visual comedy to literary dialogue and back again.

Of all the immigrant and refugee creators of movies who were fascinated by American small towns, in the years when those towns provided an important audience for the movies, none had a more bizarre relation to ordinary American life than Sturges, and none made more wholehearted, complex movies about that setting. It's hard to imagine how any native-born American could be more an outsider to the microcosm of small-town life than this nominal Chicagoan educated in Switzerland and Normandy, the only child of Mary Desti (of Frank O'Hara's poem "Mary Desti's Ass").

Born Mary Dempsey, she met a short-statured bill collector and trapeze artist from Chicago named Biden. Her marriage to this man, referred to dryly by Sturges in his memoirs as "Mr. Biden," lasted just long enough to conceive Preston, who chose to take his name from his mother's later, richest and most benign husband. Mary was the close companion of Isadora Duncan, and at times dressed her son in flowing Greek robes. She changed "Dempsey"

FIGURE 11. Preston Sturges and Eddie Bracken on the set of *The Miracle of Morgan's Creek*. Courtesy of Paramount Pictures/Photofest, Inc.

to "D'Este," and when sued in Paris by the distinguished family of that name she changed the spelling to Desti, which became the name of the salon and cosmetics business that Preston Sturges ran for a while—at the age of sixteen. The business did not thrive, but in the course of its fall Preston Sturges did invent smear-proof lipstick. Even earlier, while still a schoolboy in Switzerland, Sturges published—in Latvia!—a ragtime tune he wrote, entitled "Winky." Successful writing for the stage brought him to Hollywood as a writer, then as a director.

Unlike any Russian-born Jewish movie mogul, unlike the Europeans who came to Los Angeles fleeing the Nazis, unlike the English technician-genius Hitchcock, Sturges came to the American town from both outside and inside, with European detachment or wonder as well as American confidence that he was a native. The urbane view from outside that Faulkner creates as a matter of art, by crafting his high-perspective narrative voice, is an angle of observation that Sturges commands as a matter of manners and experience.

The bustle of the small town's public space, with frantic activity crowding the little agora, sets the tone for both of Sturges's small-town movies, *The Miracle of Morgan's Creek* and *Hail the Conquering Hero*. Both made in 1944, both movies use the same set, downtown and residential facades that look a lot like the idealized town in the Andy Hardy movies—and remarkably like the residential and downtown locations in Santa Rosa that Hitchcock uses (and for some scenes reproduces as sets) for *Shadow of a Doubt*. The downtown snarled in unaccustomed, frantic traffic in the opening scene of *Hail the Conquering Hero* could be the same Santa Rosa street where Hitchcock shows Theresa Wright's Charlie, nearly struck by car traffic, to be admonished by a protective cop (who is blind to her real danger from a homicidal uncle), when she is feeling most helplessly pressed by events.

The noisy, impatient and heedless mass energy in the two Sturges films—both made in wartime—is generated by the military. An influx of soldiers disrupts the streets

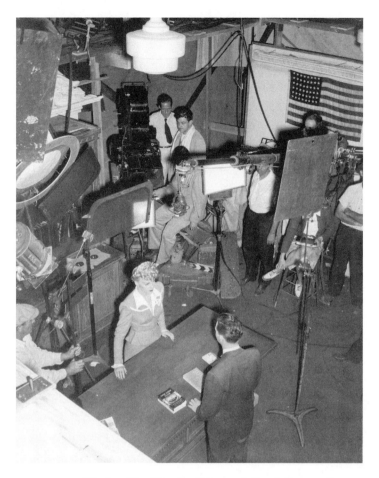

FIGURE 12. Filming *The Miracle of Morgan's Creek:* Preston Sturges directing Betty Hutton and Eddie Bracken amid the elaborate technology needed to create the familiar, homey interior of a small-town music store. Courtesy of Paramount Pictures/Photofest, Inc.

of Morgan's Creek looking for girls or, failing that, for something to do. The first conversation we witness in downtown Morgan's Creek is a traffic dispute between some of those soldiers and the constable—played by the great comic actor William Demarest, representing the old, orderly calm of the town—who is struggling franticly to control traffic. The pack of seven or eight soldiers enter a music store where, without noticing, they push aside Norval Jones when he is trying to see his girlfriend, who happens to be the constable's daughter. In keeping with the theme of the agora—and the ideas of art and commerce—the character played by Betty Hutton works in that downtown music emporium, and her admirer Norval (Eddie Bracken) is a clerk at the bank.

That the uniformed newcomers are not so much deliberately rude or arrogant as oblivious only makes it worse for Norval, who has no way to protest. An allergy has kept good-hearted, ineffectual Norval out of uniform, to his pained humiliation. In *Hail the Conquering Hero*, Bracken's very similar character Woodrow Truesmith finds himself swept along against his will by seven marines, then by a packed, confusing scene in downtown Oakdale, propelling helpless Woodrow—and us in the audience—with the hurricane force of three competing brass bands, a speech by the mayor, and a kaleidoscope of subplots bursting with characters. Woodrow like Norval wanted to be a hero in uniform: in his case the problem was hay fever. He was discharged from the Marine Corps after a month, though the marines slap a uniform on him and present him to the town as a hero.

This is the vitality of the marketplace turned monstrous as well as comical. Sturges is often described as unbelievably daring, and astonishingly deft at getting away with what he dares, and that description is just: in a war year, he made two movies in which his hero is of military age but does not serve. Sturges, in both movies, has American soldiers disrupt ordinary lives, by falsehood and by sexual recklessness; and even more remarkably he made a comedy in which an all-American girl goes dancing and is impregnated that same night by a soldier whose name she cannot quite recall. (She thinks it was something Polish, possibly Ratzkiwatzki.) There is even a slight but distinct suggestion that not one but several soldiers were involved. The rapidity of editing, the snap of dialogue, the eccentric, accelerated movement among modes, ranging from vaudeville pratfalls to verbal ironies and allusions—all the Sturges speed and smarts—bring to the small town a high-pressure risk and elation more usually associated with movies set in the big city. That rapid aesthetic footwork is part of how these movies get away with their daring material. Sturges has the formal means to suggest the way Puddn'head Wilson might laugh back at the town.

But the scandal of the pregnancy (or of pretending to be a war hero), along with Sturges's artful way of ameliorating the scandal by barrage of extenuation (bump on the head, spiked lemonade, an actual marriage ceremony, a ring of sorts, Betty Hutton's bouncy cuteness as Trudy, Bracken's patent and nebbishy earnestness as Norval) all constitute something like a stage magician's distraction, a flurry of narrative business deflecting moral attention from where the movie's blade most emphatically cuts. Even the suffering of Norval, who is willing to marry the girl—more or less bigamously—becomes a kind of side-issue. When the Hutton character is shocked at the idea of Norval as a solution, her kid sister says that he was *made* for it, "As the ox was made to eat, and the grape was made to drink."

That preposterous, flamboyant language—spoken by a child—is the elaborate right-hand gesture distracting the audience from a sneaking prestidigitation by the left—in this case, the little sister's shameless, pragmatic moral callousness. Her small-town, shrugging fatalism comes coated in the comically unlikely figurative language, vaguely biblical, of "the ox" and "the grape." Putting such dialogue credibly in his child character's precocious voice is like the way Sturges uses the virtuoso falls and grimaces of William Demarest, the child's ever-exasperated constable father: both kinds of extravagance, part of Sturges's stylistic range, seduce us toward his satirical insight. The élan of contrasts—paternal dignity with acrobatic pratfall, girlish innocence with serpentine rhetoric—helps float scandalous narrative material, like the one-night-stand or the unearned war medals, right past resistance.

The Miracle of Morgan's Creek wields a savage double edge of violation and redemption: first, there is the shallowness, even the meanness, of Morgan's Creek itself: covering the family with woe, firing Trudy's father, an upright widower, from his job as constable, a heartless community that betrays secrets and withholds mercy while self-righteously moralizing; and then there is the amiable, sublime cynicism of the *deus ex machina* that solves the problem and by a kind of offhand magic dispels the woe.

When we see the family on Christmas Eve, all is in ruin, and the town has largely shown itself to be cruel as well as stupid. The chorus we hear is like the voices of the *Our Town* dead people, but turned quicker and nastier: "He took Trudy to a Motel . . . with a false name." "What was its real name?" (Another of Sturges's nervy, disarming jokes.) "They ought to shoot him." "Maybe they will." "Shame on you Norval Jones, that'll teach you to besmirch the name of our fair city . . . lynch him."

At the culminating Town Council meeting, the town's vindictive, moralizing, and sinister element is led by Norval's employer at the Morgan's Creek Bank, Mr. Tuerck. He appears to carry the meeting, over the more benign representative of the agora, Trudy's employer at Rafferty's Music Store—a Jewish character whose immigrant accent, along with his generosity, underscores by contrast the town's Nativist nastiness or its native stupidity. And yet, as with the courtroom scene where Twain's Puddn'head Wilson sets things right, a kind of cockeyed patriotism acknowledges the town's sheltering appeal. In Dawson's Landing, the town's almost inadvertent but redeeming pluralism accepts Puddn'head; and Morgan's Creek has, as an element in its makeup, a similar pluralism represented by the immigrant Jew Rafferty.

The flagrantly artificial, beautifully acted and directed denouement—a montage including the birth of sextuplets, with Brian Donleavy and Akim Tamiroff stepping in from an earlier Sturges movie to get on the phone to fix everything with a few quick cynical strokes—rubs in the town's corruption and stupidity. Greed is added implicitly, in a culminating montage that by going around the world emphasizes the backwater nature of the town: Hitler demands a recount, newspapers in China are excited, Mussolini resigns. Donleavy and Tamiroff, the Governor and the Boss, award a retroactive commission in the State Militia. They demonstrate their worldly power to validate weddings and invalidate motels, and annul Ratzkiwatzki. "Schnook," the Boss dismisses him in a one-word speech. Norval gets his long-desired, officially approved uniform, complete with a sword of honor.

All this—"for the honor of our fair State," says the Governor—thanks to the power of publicity, and through publicity the power of money. Thus, in the last minutes of the film the Axis dictators join the newspapers of the world in saluting the Morgan's Creek sextuplets. "Canada Protests" says one of the newspaper headlines in the montage, alluding to the profits made from, though not necessarily for, the Dionne Quintuplets. Sturges's *deus ex machina* goes that actual phenomenon one better with sextuplets: a sensation or miracle that dispels the bad and inconvenient story of the drunken, disorienting night when Trudy conceived them, while her loyal boyfriend sat from evening until the next morning in front of that Main Street movie theater.

This way of resolving his movies is Sturges's benign, outsider's way of expressing what enrages Cather or Twain: the willful ignoring of history, or blindness to the larger world. The director's pleasure in leaping suddenly from Main or Broadway to the Governor's Mansion, and beyond that to China or to Mussolini's Italy, rests on Sturges's privileged viewpoint as an outsider, examining his American towns with an amused, cosmopolitan and unillusioned forgiveness. He is nearly a European, yet enough of an American to make his masterpieces epic duels between small-mindedness and innocence, resolved cynically from above.

VIII {MOONSTONE}

In *The Miracle of Morgan's Creek,* Sturges opens his story
outward and upward for its climax: into the Chinese and
Russian newspapers, and into the headquarters of indig-
nant, hysterical Hitler and dumbfounded Mussolini—the
director, with a knowing grin to his audience, hustling the
narrative onto the world stage, not by anything implicit
in his central characters or their dilemmas, but by means
of an absurdity as fantastic as his cynicism is realistic. For
a true provincial, the course from the little place into the
great world cannot be so fluently absurd or fantastic: it is
a reality, arduous and punishing, an odyssey pursued with
resolute, sometimes grim, passion.

In her life as in her work, Willa Cather, opposite to Sturges, takes that more classic course: born in Back Creek
Valley, Virginia, the oldest of seven children, she arrives
at the age of ten in Red Cloud, Nebraska. In her early
teens, she crops her hair, begins to wear men's clothing,

71

FIGURE 13. Willa Cather at seventeen, as a student in the University of Nebraska's Latin Preparatory School. Courtesy of the Bernice Slote Papers, Archives and Special Collections, University of Nebraska–Lincoln Libraries.

and follows the country physician on his rounds, signing her name "William Cather, M.D." At sixteen, she enters the University of Nebraska, where she begins publishing journalism and reviews; then she moves to Pittsburgh as a journalist for *The Home Monthly*, work that gives her access to events like Metropolitan Opera Company performances of Wagner. And she completes the American story by coming to New York.

In Pittsburgh, Cather became attached to Isabelle McClung, a well-off young woman whose family introduced Cather into Pittsburgh's artistic and elegant social life. The two young women went to Europe together, and they lived together for six years. Then, Cather left Pittsburgh for New York, by herself, to become an editor at *McClure's* magazine. Her genius, luck and resistance to ordinary norms propelled her on a trajectory from the small town to the great world embodied by the definitive Broadway of New York.

Cather chose to tell that story indirectly, in a way unlike conventional autobiographical fiction. The artist in *The Song of the Lark* is a musician not a writer, and the details of the character's singing career are not based on Cather's life. However, the journey from an obscure settlement to the famous stages of the world is Cather's story, along with the erotic pressures, sacrifices and distortions of that artist's journey. The heroic scale of Cather's narrative, and its heroic force, may emanate partly from the demanding quality of invention that the novel's transformations— from writing to music, from the author's sexuality to the character's—demanded of Cather. The story of Thea Kronborg, along with that central character, makes its way out of her home town Moonstone and above it, into the world's great capitals—with a propulsive conviction derived from the town Thea escapes, and that the narrative returns to repeatedly. The town's name suggests an amulet or fetish, a moonstone possibly worthless in itself, or bewitched, but capable of guiding and preserving the one who keeps it in her grasp.

Or, "Moonstone" suggests unreality, falseness, reflected rather than original energy, or the absence of much to value in a bit of feldspar, a semiprecious pebble. Nevertheless, Dawson or Grover or Morgan or the Frenchman or the Wine of Winesburg, Ohio, merely happened to be first to stop at some nothing of a locale, and in those instances the

73

place has lacked the imagination or distinction to supersede its first, casual, or perfunctory label of convenience. "Moonstone" in contrast is mysterious and romantic, however ironically. The name also suggests that the place is as cut off from human history as a meteor, the town no more Swedish or Spanish or Indian or anything else than a fragment of lunar or lunatic rock.

"Moonstone" like those names made of possessives, expresses not only a craving for historical reality, but its frustration: a lack of density, or a failure of the process celebrated by Bishop Berkeley's "Verses on the Prospect of Planting Arts and Learning in America." Beyond colonization, Berkeley—the California university town is named for him, in recognition of this poem—writes envisioning a vigorous New World surpassing the exhausted Old, going beyond it in knowledge and imagination. The poem, best known for the line "Westward the course of empire takes its way," begins:

> The Muse, disgusted at an age and clime
> Barren of every glorious theme,
> In distant lands now waits a better time,
> Producing subjects worthy fame:

The eighteenth-century philosopher entertains the idea that raw new settlements may produce glory, worthy of fame, on a scale lost to the exhausted Old World. Dawson and Grover, like Woodrow Truesmith's grandfather, may or may not be worthy of fame. In keeping with Berkeley's vision, Thea Kronborg, most emphatically, is worthy of fame and attains it.

74

The Sturges films and Cather's *The Song of the Lark* portray diametrically opposite versions of the hero or extraordinary person: the whole point of Sturges's people is how ordinary they are, epitomized by Eddie Bracken's easily flustered, allergy-ridden, malleable characters. Betty Hutton's lip-synching to a *basso profundo* recording, from behind the music store counter, early in *The Miracle of Morgan's Creek* emphasizes how she is, really, just a local gal lively enough to pretend she is something else—in gender, among other things. In contrast Cather's book, perhaps the most impressive American narrative about the life of an artist, is based entirely on the idea of a person who is extraordinary. Sexual mores and gender expectations, comically malleable in *The Miracle of Morgan's Creek,* are serious, even menacing forces for Cather.

For Sturges, art appears as a candid, open manipulation, displayed to make a comic point, as when those cynical characters imported from an earlier movie (*The Great McGinty*), the equivalent of unlikely gods from the sky, appear to solve and resolve everything at the very end of *Morgan's Creek.* In *Hail the Conquering Hero* the artificial solution is an implausible mass change of heart, a fit of generosity by the town itself. "There's something rotten in our town," says the Judge, and the script happily dismantles the place's judgment, dismantles even the idea of heroism: "He's a *hero,*" says the Sergeant: "He's got a statue in the park, and the birds sit on him."

As to the electoral process, when Woodrow objects to the lies the marines are telling everyone about his entirely fabricated exploits in battle, the Sergeant explains, with a tone of affronted virtue:

Who's telling lies . . . ? Every one of those boys is telling the truth . . . except they change the names a little so's not to give out military information. Lies! Anyway those ain't lies . . . those is campaign promises . . . they expect those!

The sweet, sincere patriotism of the ordinary home town boy (named "Norval" or "Truesmith," suggesting not only the normal and the true but the nearly anonymous plainness of "Smith") in both of these movies preserves the affection expressed by the domestic and downtown architecture, the small bits of social comedy, the family life and home cooking and neighborliness—all existing in a contradictory balance with the literal and figurative propensity to lynch. Woodrow Truesmith expresses convincing, deep loyalty to the town of Oakdale, where he sold papers and would love to be mayor, and which was once his grandfather's farm.

Not so Thea Kronborg of Moonstone. Cather makes it her business to fill in the town's texture in evocative detail, but the singer Kronborg's story moves her beyond her birthplace, to the great cities. The richly imagined, dense reality of Moonstone, its half-dead but stubborn tendrils reaching back in time to Europe and to pre-Columbian dwellings, provides the setting for Cather's story of the artist who comes from the town, and the ways she is of it and not of it.

Thea's childhood mentor Dr. Archie says of his collected Balzac, "They aren't exactly books, Thea . . . they're a city." The girl says, "A history, you mean?" He answers with what I take to be Cather's credo regarding her own art: "Yes and no. They're a history of a live city, not a

FIGURE 14. Eddie Bracken, Ella Raines and William Demarest in Sturges's *Hail the Conquering Hero*. Uniforms, a pretty girl, a picket fence, a convertible car, a leafy street, flowers for a celebration: in the movie's story, the emotions these things generate are built on a lie—and survive the lie. Courtesy of Paramount Pictures/Photofest, Inc.

dead one. . . . You'll like to read it some day, when you're grown up."

Then they have a dialogue that raises more or less directly the question of an epitomizing microcosm: does each place epitomize the world, or are the differences between, say, Moonstone and Paris, differences of kind? Dr. Archie, reader of Balzac in the American Plains, leans toward the idea of the universal; but the ambitious Thea, while still too young to realize how ambitious she is, takes a different view. He observes that she is always curious about people, and Balzac understood people very well. Thea responds with a question:

> "City people or country people?"
> "Both. People are pretty much the same everywhere."
> "Oh, no, they're not. The people who go through in the dining-car aren't like us."
> "What makes you think they aren't, my girl? Their clothes?"
> Thea shook her head. "No, it's something else. I don't know." [Then she glances at the row of uniformly bound volumes and asks him,] "How soon will I be old enough to read them?"

Cather doesn't so much settle the question whether people are "pretty much the same everywhere" as expand it, so that the young artist's perception of social differences—she is based on the soprano Olive Fremstad, a celebrated artist Cather interviewed and got to know, perhaps loved—becomes a token of her destiny to see more, learn more, discriminate more, than any surroundings at all could supply. She confirms the doctor's sense of things to some extent when she first comes to Chicago, with its celebrated *virtuosi* and imposing concert halls, including Louis Sullivan's splendid Auditorium. In the city, the established sopranos—women older than Thea, with large followings and breathless praise in the press—turn out to be not very good musically. Their shallow charms or middlebrow poses, expertly deployed and commended, remind her of the cute, mediocre girl who was her competition in church performances back home: "Chicago was not so very different from Moonstone, after all, and Jessie Darcey was only Lily Fisher under another name." This equivalence of the cosmopolitan and the provincial is, in a way, the ultimate disillusionment: there is no reliable context for the artist, no assizes in the world, great or small, commensurate with art itself.

Cather writes a great novel about an artist while also writing a great work about the provincial American town. The two themes enrich one another. One might say that the intruder, the outsider, in *The Song of the Lark*, unlike Faulkner's Snopes or Sturges's marines, is the spirit of art itself—except that Cather discloses, within her town of Moonstone, both genuine art and the hunger for art—however clumsy or frail its expression. Just as Chicago turns out to harbor provinciality and plausible mediocrity, Moonstone turns out to harbor seeds of high art.

Cather is endlessly informative and funny about the taste for lame or semi-lame or overestimated poetry recited at the turn of the previous century. Including actual examples of taste, she tells us about reproductions of admired genteel pictures, such as a "military allegory" by F. B. Wigle called *Drummer Boy of Shiloh*. She alludes to the career of the immensely popular Maggie Mitchell, playing her ingenue role into her seventies, in the blockbuster hit play *Little Barefoot* by Augustus Waldauer. A cold, all-but-dispirited dread, an emotion beyond melancholy and above the comic stupidity of respectable taste, runs through Cather's accounts of successful bad art. In *My Ántonia*, the drifter who commits suicide by leaping into a thresher turns out to have in his pocket a copy of Samuel Woodworth's "The Old Oaken Bucket," an extremely popular poem—when verse provided its era with the equivalent of our own country-and-western music—of sentimental nostalgia for a childhood home. Genuine art, in contrast, comes to Thea's native town of Moonstone mainly by way of immigrants and misfits, such as Wunsch, her first music teacher. Thea's own family are Swedish immigrants. When she reads aloud for Wunsch, in German, Heinrich Heine's poem "Am leuchtenden Sommermorgen," he becomes agitated—upset because he hears, in the child's understated, musical way of saying the verses, *der Geist, die Phantasie, der Rhythmus*. Her voice when she says the poem is "no longer the voice which spoke the speech of Moonstone." The reality of art, realized in Thea's voice, confronts Wunsch with all his levels and forms of exile. He begins talking to himself, not to Thea, about how much she will be capable of learning. "*Aber nicht die Americanischen Fräulein,*" he mutters, "They are like the ones in the *Märchen*, a grinning face and hollow in the insides."

Wunsch's agitated recognition of spirit, imagination, rhythm, in his student presages his collapse into drink. He is a disastrous alcoholic, eventually destroying himself utterly. His denial of inner life to Americans—with the American girl there before him who plays so well, who responds to Ovid and Heine as well as to Mozart and Verdi—is a kind of confession on Wunsch's part. He cannot survive in this country, though he senses that Thea can—even though she is an artist. Dr. Archie, with his volumes of Balzac, is also a melancholy figure, and also an outsider or newcomer to Moonstone. Like Wunsch he too feels "the fear of the tongue, that terror of little towns."

In contrast with those figures who despair and sink in the marketplace of American life, Thea Kronborg's Chicago teacher Harsanyi has survived his child-prodigy years of exploitation by his father, and survives also his immigrant experience in America. In the Pennsylvania mining town where he grew up, an explosion destroyed some of the shanties where Harsanyi's family lived, and cost him an eye. But unlike Wunsch, Harsanyi becomes an American, even though the New World agora he experiences may be less a meeting-place than a "scramble":

> He still had a clipping from a Pittsburgh paper, giving a list of the dead and injured. He appeared as "Harsanyi, Andor, left eye and slight injuries about the head." That was his first American "notice"; and he kept it. He held no grudge against the coal company; he understood that the accident was merely one of the things that are bound to happen in the general scramble of American life, where every one comes to grab and takes his chance.

Possibly the most impressive artist in Moonstone is Spanish Johnny, a figure significant not only because of his uncanny musical ability but because he comes from a Mexican community within Moonstone. Faulkner, in *The Hamlet*'s inferior sequel *The Town*, alludes briefly to Jefferson's Chinese laundryman and two "Jew brothers" with clothing stores, one of them learned in Greek and Latin. Faulkner even discloses that the sewing machine agent V. K. Ratliff gets his initials from a Russian ancestor, Vladimir Kirilovich. Sturges in his movies of small-town life includes ethnic types, such as the saintly Jewish music store keeper Mr. Rafferty.

Cather's Moonstone, small though it is, has a district known as Mexican Town, with a few dozen families, and Thea goes to a dance there, in an adobe hall. Spanish Johnny is as tormented and erratic in his own way as Wunsch, and more than a little crazy—sometimes Johnny plays with demonic energy, to tremendous applause, then undergoes a seizure or manic collapse. He has "spells." But on this summer evening in Mexican Town he is an elegant host and colleague. His community is possibly idealized by Cather, but not excessively. The Mexican-Americans of Moonstone are presented with conviction, in detail. The musicians of the community have violins, and even a double bass. Late in an evening that Cather makes convincingly idyllic, Thea sings while Spanish Johnny plays. The telling of this moment is ecstatic, even sexualized:

> She had sung for churches and funerals and teachers, but she had never before sung for a really musical people, and this was the first time she had ever felt the response that such people can give. They turned themselves and all they had over to her. For the moment they cared about nothing in the world but what she was doing. Their faces confronted her, open, eager, unprotected. She felt as if all these warm-blooded people débouched into her. Mrs. Tellamantez's fateful resignation, Johnny's madness, the adoration of the boy who lay still in the sand; in an instant these things seemed to be within her instead of without, as if they had come from her in the first place.

Here is an unexpected sense of fulfillment, in an American town, in an experience with art at the center of it. What seemed to be outside is inside. What was inside is made available, and accepted by the audience that is described as "unprotected" as well as eager. We are far here from gossip and repression, the terrible fear of the tongue—though this expedition of Thea's does draw attention from the nasty tongues of Moonstone, the equivalents of the Morgan's Creek citizens who want to shoot or lynch the Eddie Bracken character because they believe he took his girl to a motel.

Thea Kronborg will return to Chicago after this evening of music among the Mexicans of Moonstone, and she will go on to New York and to the cities of Europe. In this moment of her narrative, the elusive, easily abused spirit of art harbors in Moonstone itself. A German immigrant couple, the Kohlers, hear from their house Thea's voice joining in a Mexican part-song, then at the appointed moment in the sextet from *Lucia di Lammermoor*. "At the appointed, at the acute moment," Thea's voice shoots up "like a fountain jet" into the light, above the male voices "like a goldfish darting among creek minnows." Fritz Kohler nods to his wife: "*Ja*," he says "*schön*."

Wunsch and Spanish Johnny, the immigrant, disreputable misfits, are beacons for Thea within Moonstone. But her strongest vision of art is historical, American and ancient—embodying a remote past, a reverse of the time capsule that the citizens in *Our Town* put under the cornerstone of their bank, looking hopefully toward a remote future. The book's definitive vision of art comes when Thea is in Arizona, among the pueblos of the cliff-dwelling Ancient People. The shards of pottery water jugs in the cave where she sleeps have a sacred quality for her. These surviving fragments of shaped and baked earth are beautifully decorated: "This care, expended upon vessels

83

which could not hold food or water any better for the additional labor put upon them, made her heart go out to those ancient potters." The aesthetic, expressive element in these pre-Colombian potsherds moves Thea in relation to the useful, vital function of the objects for the Ancient People:

> all their customs and ceremonies and religion went back to water. . . . Their pottery was their most direct appeal to water, the envelope and sheath of the precious element itself. The strongest Indian need was expressed in those graceful jars, fashioned slowly by hand, without the aid of a wheel.

Thea has been in a crisis regarding her music and her voice. When she bathes in the waterfall below the caves, the water suggests the realization that her voice, like the water vessels, is a sheath for the fluid, elusive element of breath, of life itself. Also involved is a connection to the past: "Those potsherds were like fetters, that bound one to a long chain of human endeavor."

Finally, this vision of continuity, and of a social place where art and usefulness conjoin with communal life, completes Thea's, and Cather's, rejection of Moonstone. She says of the town's complacency, its resistance to what she calls "any serious effort": "No more of that! The Cliff Dwellers had lengthened the past. She had older and higher obligations."

In other words, she comes to a definition of the adequate community that extends vertically in time, farther into the past that the town has conceived. The novel's last words envision that vertical, temporal ideal extended forward into the future too. Thea's proud, admiring Aunt

FIGURE 15. Willa Cather's Red Cloud, Nebraska. Courtesy of Webster County Historical Museum, Red Cloud, Nebraska.

Tillie tells the young people in Moonstone, in her silly way, about Thea's attainment in art and the world. Cather's last sentences are about those stories Aunt Tillie tells. The passage presents a notion of culture, an idea about the nature of quiet little places in her country, and specifically about their wants. As with the ancient pottery of the cliff dwellers, the image involves the lifegiving, ever changing element of water:

> The many naked little sandbars which lie between Venice and the mainland, in the seemingly stagnant water of the lagoons, are made habitable and wholesome only because, every night, a foot and a half of tide creeps in from the sea and winds its fresh brine up through all that network of shining water-ways. So, into all the little settlements of quiet people, tidings of what their boys and girls are doing in the world bring real refreshment; bring to the old, memories, and to the young, dreams.

85

IX {LONG BRANCH}

My home town may not exactly fit the subject of provincial American towns, because Long Branch is such an extraordinary place. Or, is that feeling part of my chauvinism, or nostalgia?

I began this consideration of the town as it appears in certain works by disavowing nostalgia, that merely sentimental longing: a response to change so purely regretful that it is generic and cottony—lacking substance no matter how freighted it may be with specific, tender details. In fact, the very intensity of the details may manifest the puffed, spun-sugar nature of the feeling. Loss is real. Elegy, recognizing loss, measures the weight of change; nostalgia is nearly weightless. Such is the traditional, strict distinction: nostalgia is a blurry retrospective gaze in the wake of change; loss is loss.

A worthwhile distinction, though in practice it is not always clear. Court decisions have affirmed that the First

Amendment rights that apply to the public space of a town do not exist in the private space of the shopping mall. That represents a loss, nostalgia aside. On the other hand, the Constitution does not, in the narrated event, prevent the lynching performed by the citizens of Dawson's Landing, as imagined by Mark Twain, and reflecting many decades of countless actual lynchings. It also might be that the human scale of downtown promotes civility, as the anonymity of the mall—let alone the World Wide Web—cannot. But that human scale does not seem to make the vengeful citizens of Moonstone or Morgan's Creek less vicious or opprobrious.

The playing out of change in a place, and our outraged or elegiac gaze back at it, are fountains of ambiguity. It is change that gives such places their meaning: change in the places; in the country they belong to; and in the people who leave the town behind, then for the rest of their lives reflect back on it—as those others who remain in the place all of their years, absorbing its changes and participating in them, may not. Puddn'head Wilson and Thea Kronborg become curatorial of their towns as they once were. Citizens more embedded in a place may forget more easily, or may find that forgetting is a practical requirement.

Here is a specific image or myth of change from the history of Long Branch, from before I was born. As a summer resort town, Long Branch has been elegiac on different levels of time. As implacable as the wheel of the tides, the cycle of the year regularly subdues the oceanfront boardwalk and hotels. The honky-tonk flowering of a seaside vacation spot in summer, the Season, is briefer than the long, lonely annual sleep that surrounds it.

On a larger scale, the town has for over a century told itself that it has seen better days. It could be argued that in Long Branch the idea of celebrity was born: the nineteenth-century upper classes, vessels of the obsolete idea of Society, went to Newport or Saratoga Springs. To raffish Long Branch, closer to New York, came the less-respectable, gaudy show business people, the climbers and patent medicine millionaires who have inherited the world. To Long Branch, the gambler Diamond Jim Brady brought Lillian Russell. Brady designed and commissioned an electric car with a rounded glass front, with no headlights but a hundred bulbs in that transparent interior, where the couple could seat themselves on display, two large-bodied people adorned with brocades and sparkling jewelry, gliding silently at dusk down the oceanfront promenade, trailed by a procession of spare cars, each chauffeured and ready to serve in case of mechanical failure.

That image—Brady and Russell in a silent yet mobile display, illuminated like figures in a store window, their electric chariot a harbinger of the coming century—comes from a book by Judge Alton Evans: *Entertaining a Nation: The Career of Long Branch,* published by the Writers' Project of the Works Project Administration in 1940. Judge Evans, writing from the viewpoint of the Great Depression, regarded a town that had gone into its own economic decline before the rest of the country. The Long Branch of presidents and Winslow Homer, the time of Phil Daly and Diamond Jim Brady, had faded. By the thirties, the hotels, the Boardwalk amusements, the dance palaces and clam bars and frozen custard stands, all depended on Italian and Jewish vacationers.

On July 2, 1924—at the height of the Season, when the town's population was each year doubled for a few months by summer visitors—the Ku Klux Klan held a tristate Konklave in Long Branch's Elkwood Park. This was no small get-together. As the climax to the Konklave, the assembled Klansmen staged a Fourth of July parade, a march down Broadway of so many be-sheeted figures that, according to Judge Evans, the procession "took four hours to pass a given spot." In his words:

> the effect on Long Branch business was disastrous. The Jewish summer residents departed from the town the next day practically *en masse,* leaving a deserted city of ruined shopkeepers and empty hotels and boarding houses. The Negro population locked its doors tight and refused to emerge on the streets for several days. Similarly, Catholics, for whose benefit several fiery crosses had been burned, either left the community or took steps to protect themselves.

The clarity and elegance of the prose, along with the dry understatement of little writerly moments like "for whose benefit," are admirable.

This narrative, like much in Judge Evans's book, overlaps with lore known by word of mouth, with many elaborations and variants. My family had its own version of a particular anecdote about the Klan parade. Judge Evans writes:

> A group of three nuns associated with the Star of the Sea Academy saw the parade, and as one robed and hooded figure passed, the trio exclaimed as they saw his feet, "The iceman." That individual received no more orders from either

the academy or its neighboring Catholic institutions. Several weeks later a sheepish iceman confirmed their guess when he called to inquire whether they had stopped taking ice "just because I was in that parade."

The forces of intimacy and alienation in this episode remind me of the same elements as imagined by American artists from Twain to Sturges—the town as a little theater for the historical forces of Church and Klan, the name "Star of the Sea" reaching far away in time and space. Here too are the anonymous disguise in a sinister mass, the recognition that precedes and justifies rejection, the "sheepish" inquiry with its plea for redemption, based on something different from merit or extenuation: "Just because I was in that parade." This mild, homey and deprecating approach by the iceman is in its way the most horrible and characteristic element in the story: a plea that here in our little community, whatever is symbolized by the burning cross cannot much matter, though it might be serious elsewhere.

My mother told the story differently. In her version, a certain high school teacher and athletic coach had been recognized as one of the hooded marchers, by his distinctive shoes. She told me that she recognized those shoes herself. This man was still teaching American History in Long Branch High School thirty years later—one of several teachers who as young beginners taught my parents and then, on the brink of retirement years later, my brother and sister and me. Only after graduation did I consider that my mother, never a reliable reporter, was seven years old at the time of the Ku Klux Klan parade down Broadway. The chronology is possible—the young man sucked

FIGURE 16. July 2, 1924: a Konklave of Ku Klux Klan members from three states parade down Broadway in Long Branch, New Jersey. The head of the parade, with the flag, is at the exact location of Dr. Alexander Vineburg's optometry office, where Milford Pinsky began working when he was in high school, remaining there until Dr. Vineburg fired him in 1947, shortly after the birth of Milford's second child. The tail of the parade, quite far up Broadway, must be close to Dave Pinsky's bar, the Broadway Tavern. Courtesy of Brown Brothers, Sterling, Pennsylvania.

into the KKK and its parade, the child seeing or more likely hearing from gossip about those telltale shoes, the former marcher teaching her and then her children thirty-odd years later as the generations proceeded—though unlikely. Whatever the literal case, the compression of time in my mother's imagination discloses an essential truth.

Proximity in time is like a province of its own. Someone may have imagined that coach's youthful parading with the Klan, or deliberately invented it—the "terror of the tongues" indeed. Conceivably, it happened, just as

Sylvia Pinsky told me it did. But like the more sober imagination of Judge Alton Evans, her narrative belongs in a close web of strands that include D. W. Griffith's *The Birth of a Nation*, the first American feature film, with its heroic Klansmen, released nine years before the Tri-State Konklave—that is, in 1915, the same year that Cather published *The Song of the Lark*. Veterans and widows of the American Civil War were still alive, in Long Branch and elsewhere, and could read the novel or see the movie. The Republic had come apart not so long before.

The historical web in American time is manifold and intricate, yet small. The handsome, charismatic Garfield was shot in a Washington train station on July 2, planning to spend the summer with his family in Long Branch. Suffering from his wound and likely killed by the stream of doctors poking at it, each eager for prestige and each with unwashed hands, Garfield lingered in the White House through record heat. The Potomac swamps grew malarial. Engineers hung the White House with sheets soaked in ice water, and directed fans across them.

Finally, in early September, the President's mattress was carried from the White House into a railroad carriage fitted with special springs. In Long Branch, hundreds of men worked all night to lay a railroad spur from the Elberon Station to the door of the Francklyn cottage on the oceanfront, five-eighths of a mile away. People came from the hotels with coffee and sandwiches for the workers. (A Captain Mount, who had fought for the Confederacy, refused to take part in the work, then relented and worked when he learned that the President was a fellow Mason.) The next day, Garfield's carriage made its way along the new spur to the cottage where he is said to have been made comfortable by the ocean breezes. He died a couple of weeks later.

In his account from which I have raided these details, Judge Evans makes a small-town gesture. He writes of the railway spur, and the special light engine that took the president's car along it from station to cottage:

> The important work of guiding the car to its final destination was entrusted to engineer Dan Mansfield and fireman Martin Maloney, both of whom died recently in Long Branch.

The specific names, the words "recently in Long Branch," the small span of time and space that stands for the horror and heroism of Civil War, assassination, scandal and generosity, the venoms and comforts of any specific little place—the sentence is simple and dignified without solemnity or self-importance. A reader is free to imagine a touch in it somewhere of an awareness, too gentle for irony, that these two men are small on the great stage of events, but considerable in their town. To mediate between those two scales of importance has been the labor of great imaginations.

ACKNOWLEDGMENTS

I am grateful to Rice University for inviting me to give the inaugural Campbell Lectures, and for the generosity of my welcome at Rice when I presented this book in its early form. In particular, I thank Dean of Humanities Gary Wihl for his graciousness. The Campbell family were hospitable, warm and intellectually attentive, as were Robert Patten, Edward Snow, Susan Wood and many other members of the Rice faculty.

Formal and informal discussions at Rice with such colleagues were instructive, as well as encouraging and lively. Sarah Campbell, for example, directed me to a significant passage in Cather's *Song of the Lark*.

Valued readers who helped me make the lectures into a book include: Frank Bidart, Louise Glück, Stephen Greenblatt, Ha Jin, Ellen Pinsky, Nicole Pinsky, Lloyd Schwartz and Tom Sleigh. Karen Broderick's skill and judgment were essential to finding and assembling the illustrations. Brandy Barents was a wise and efficient helper.

In another way I am indebted to family, friends and neighbors from my home town, Long Branch, New Jersey. My brother Richard Pinsky and my sister Susan Pinsky have provided inspiration, as have our many Long Branch cousins and aunts and uncles, especially uncle Martin Penn, aunt Thelma Tarantola, aunt Dorothy Wright and her friend Bill Cole: Long Branch High School alumni all. Also other Long Branch people: Meyer Abrams, Phylis Asch Cobianchi, Joan Bartee, Greg and Marina Christopher, Joe Cittadino, Joanie DiSheplo, Connie Lawn, Mike Lubetkin, Carly Mehler, Frank Pallone, Adam Schneider, Joe Talarico, Jean Vandermark Lomet, Charlie Vitola, and Jerry Wolfson. (I could go on.)